Lola T70

V8 COUPÉS

A TECHNICAL APPRAISAL

Lola T70
V8 COUPÉS

A TECHNICAL APPRAISAL

IAN BAMSEY

Foulis

Haynes

A **FOULIS** MOTORING BOOK

First published 1990

Published by:
Haynes Publishing Group
Sparkford, Near Yeovil, Somerset BA22 7JJ
England

Haynes Publications Inc.
861 Lawrence Drive, Newbury Park,
California, 91320, USA

Produced for GT Foulis & Co. Ltd. by
RACECAR ENGINEERING
(Racecar Engineering Specialist Publications)
Telephone or Fax (0935) 31295
Editorial Director: Ian Bamsey
Research Assistant: Alan Lis

British Library Cataloguing in Publication
Data
Bamsey, Ian
Lola T70 - Aston Martin & Chevrolet coupes.
1. Racing cars, history
I. Title
629.22809

ISBN 0-85429-839-8

Library of Congress Catalog
Card number 90-83291

Printed in England by:
J. H. Haynes & Co. Ltd.
Typesetting & Artwork by:
Photosetting, Yeovil, Somerset

INTRODUCTION

In 1967 the Lola T70 had a baptism of fire, unleashing its five hundred horses onto the dauntingly fast sweeps of the Spa Francorchamps road circuit. It was a dream to drive, even the awesome flat out Masta kink no terror trip. Two years later the equally potent Porsche 917 had its initiation at Francorchamps and was a nightmare.

By 1969 Sports-Prototypes were limited to 5.0 litres and the pushrod Chevrolet in the Lola was then at a major disadvantage against the 12 cylinder race engine designed specifically for the challenging new Porsche. In spite of that, at Francorchamps and through the high speed curves of the Osterreichring the T70 could hold its own. It was not until after the Osterreichring race that Porsche discovered the way of successful Sports-Prototype chassis design. Which was to copy the aerodynamics of the Lola T70.

The T70 was a superb chassis lacking a competitive engine. Nevertheless, it is remembered as a classic among Sports-Prototypes, largely for widespread success in the shorter, non-championship events with which the undependable Chevrolet engine could cope. In technical terms, it was a very important motor car, contributing a great deal to the development of the fully enclosed mid engine coupe at a time of significant change in both tyre technology and aerodynamic practice.

For a proper insight into its contribution, the author is particularly indebted to its creator Eric Broadley for his kind co-operation. Valuable assistance was also provided by Lola employees Laurie Bray and Terry Hadley, both of whom worked with the car in its heyday. Lola Cars Ltd Managing Director Mike Blanchet kindly arranged for the company to provide the fullest co-operation, so important in a work of this nature.

Information was also culled from a number of other individuals and various publications and special mention is due of London magazines Motor Sport and Autosport and Paris magazine Sport Auto for the excellent sporting records their back issues provide. The photographs in this book are from the archives of LAT (London Art Tech), Standard House, Bonhill Street, London EC2A 4DA.

BACKGROUND

American Aims

The Ferrari 250GT was a Gran Turismo, the Ferrari Testa Rossa was a sports-racer. The distinction between those two breeds of competition sports car was quite clear and unequivocal in the late Fifties. A Gran Turismo had a roof and could be driven on shopping errands as well as in races while a sports-racer was effectively a Grand Prix car with two seats and its wheels enclosed. Racing was its sole purpose. There was no confusion until the powers that be decided it would be a good idea to restrict international sports car racing to Gran Turismo machinery.

There were two major complications. Firstly, it was not possible to define exactly what constituted a Gran Turismo without legislating against progress. Secondly, the organisers of the classic sports car races did not want to lose the spectacle associated with sports-racing cars. Thus was born the so called 'Experimental GT' class of 1962 which sired the Project 212 Aston Martin and a 4.0 litre Testa Rossa. The former was closely related to the marque's production cars and was consequently in the spirit of Gran Turismo racing, the latter was an imposter, fooling nobody with its token road equipment but eligible for the ill defined class none the less.

Given manufacturers' desire to win races outright, the Experimental GT class encouraged the masquerader and with the development of the large capacity mid engined car in the early Sixties confusion reigned. The forerunners of this new breed had been 1961 Ferrari and Maserati spyders clearly derived from their respective Testa Rossa and Birdcage stablemates. Maserati quickly reverted to a proven front engine location but Ferrari continued to develop the central power plant theme, its '62 V6 and V8 examples sporting a token high windscreen, lights, spare wheel and luggage space for Experimental GT status.

At Le Mans in '62 the 2.5 litre V6 mid engined Ferrari traded the lead with the winning 4.0 litre Testa Rossa until its transmission broke. Meanwhile, less successful was the first large capacity mid engined car to sport a coupe body - the 2.5 litre Coventry Climax-Tojeiro entered by Ecurie Ecosse. This machine had Cooper Formula One transmission and a racing car style spaceframe chassis clothed in a pretty shell which was reminiscent of one of the Scottish team's D Types carrying a hard top. Following the philosophy of the day, it was shaped to split the air like a bullet with scant attention paid to aerodynamic theory.

The interesting Tojeiro was followed by a coupe constructed by a Grand Prix manufacturer and featuring the very latest in Formula One technology, the monocoque chassis. This was Eric Broadley's Lola Mk.VI GT. The Lola was equipped with a 4.3 litre Ford Fairlane V8 Indy engine and had Formula One-style running gear including a rear mounted gearbox (a Colotti four-speeder) in unit with the final drive, outboard disc brakes and wishbone and coil spring independent suspension front and rear. All the mechanicals were clothed in an attractive non-structural g.r.p. body, of which the lines were not dissimilar to those of the Tojeiro.

Lola Cars Ltd. of Bromley, Kent was a young company, having been formed in 1958 to productionise a club racing Special devised by Broadley, a quantity surveyor. This Lola Mk.I continued in production right up until 1962 and in the meantime the company branched into single seater racing. A front engined Formula Junior car of 1960 was followed by mid engined Formula Junior and Formula One cars for the '61 - '63 seasons (Mk.III - Mk.V) all these designs having conventional spaceframe chassis.

In '62 Broadley observed that available American V8 engines offered the right combination of performance and compact size to make a logical base for a mid engined GT racing car. He was particularly attracted by the Ford Fairlane pushrod V8 since Ford was launching a major new motorsports initiative. Indeed, in late '62 Ford signed an agreement with Lotus for a Fairlane powered Indy Car version of the monocoque Formula One machine with which Colin Chapman had astonished the racing world earlier that season.

Inspired by the Lotus 25, Lola's first monocoque chassis for the Mk.VI was based on a three-quarter length tub which ran from just behind the front wheels to the gearbox. In Lotus style, the tub was formed as a pair of longitudinal torsion boxes carrying the fuel and linked by various other chassis elements. These were a tubular sub assembly at the front (this carrying the front suspension and the radiator), a stressed skin floor, a firewall bulkhead cum roll bar and a substantial rear crossmember embracing the transmission (this carrying the rear suspension).

Flanking the cockpit and engine bay, the torsion boxes formed the fuel tanks and ran back as far as the rear wheels to support the engine, which had to be carried unstressed in view of its production base. The monocoque tub offered high torsional rigidity thanks to the generous cross-sectional area of the torsion boxes together with their firm location in relation to one another. Further, the torsion boxes provided massive beam stiffness. The boxes were complex fabrications of composite steel and aluminium panelling over magnesium formers. They were sealed with a rubber compound to hold the fuel without the need for the aircraft-type bags employed by the Lotus 25.

The use of a rigid monocoque chassis together with fully independent suspension via wishbones and coil springs front and rear for proper wheel control was highly significant at this time. Racing car tyres were improving in leaps and bounds. In the Fifties there had been little difference between road and racing tyres and this had made it feasible to produce a genuine dual purpose road and track car. However, in the early Sixties Dunlop developed a new generation of racing tyre which made gravity defying cornering a reality.

The new Dunlop tyre had a nylon rather than the traditional cotton carcase and a synthetic rather than natural rubber tread. This allowed the tread to be softer, thereby offering a higher level of grip. Where a rigid chassis and proper wheel control permitted, in the early Sixties Formula One cornering forces exceeded 1.0g for the first time ever. Heavier and having a higher centre of gravity, sports-racing cars could not quite keep up but the need for precise wheel control was no less pressing if the maximum potential was to be wrung from the new tyre technology.

The advanced Lola was designed as a very small car with little overhang front or rear and a wheelbase measuring 2356mm, less than that of the marque's contemporary 1.5 litre Grand Prix car. That made it light and manoeuvrable. Aerodynamically Broadley's GT was conventional having a full width raked windscreen behind which the roof blended into a gently sloping rear shroud that ended in a cut off 'Kamm' tail. The entire tail shroud was quickly detachable for ease of access, as was the streamlined nose with its forward-set radiator inlet and perspex headlight fairings. The lower flanks of the body were formed by the outer walls of the monocoque which curved inward in conventional sports car style.

While the Ford-Lola was a fashionable mid engined Gran Turismo in appearance (it didn't look out of place alongside an E-Type Jaguar roadster, for example), if pure racing car under the skin, the rival Ferrari continued as a traditional sports-racing car in form as well as function. Not that the so called 250P V12 machine of 1963 was necessarily any better aerodynamically than the Lola thanks to its mandatory high windscreen. The open, so called 'spyder-bodied' sports-racing cars of the Fifties of which the Ferrari was a survivor had been designed as enclosed wheel versions of contemporary Formula One cars enjoying a very low frontal area, the driver crouching behind a tiny aero screen.

Since 1960 it had been mandatory for all racing sports cars to have a high and full width windscreen. Thus the frontal area of the spyders increased massively and with it the drag produced by the car since drag is a product of a non-dimensional drag co-efficient and frontal area. Behind its mandatory windscreen the 250P's cockpit was open and its rear deck was a flat surface at wheel arch height, in usual spyder style. In contrast, Maserati had produced a version of its classic 'Birdcage' with a high rear deck, at windscreen height and a matching long and gently raked screen that extended across the bonnet. The idea was to make the car more slippery, to reduce its co-efficient of drag.

Historically, Ferrari had never put much emphasis upon aerodynamics. However, the arrival of Carlo Chiti at Maranello had focused more thought upon the subject. Significantly, at the end of the 250P's deck was a so called spoiler or vertical tab, this aerodynamic device characteristic of Ferrari sports-racers and GT cars since '61. It was nothing to do with streamlining in any conventional sense but had everything to do with the airflow.

Richie Ginther is credited with the invention of the spoiler. At Monza he found the rear end of his V6 spyder going light at speed, making the car a handful to drive through the fast, sweeping 'Curva Grande' after the pits. He suggested a vertical strip of aluminium be fitted at the end of the rear deck to well up the airflow, thus creating a local high pressure area. In theory this would counteract the tail lift - and in practice it worked. Clearly, however, with a high windscreen sweeping air over and above the rear deck - as in the case of the 250P - a spoiler could not work as effectively as it otherwise might.

Enter Michael May. May was a very clever engineer and a racing enthusiast. In the mid Fifties young Michael and cousin Pierre May raced a small capacity mid engined Porsche spyder. This arrived at the Nurburgring for the 1956 1000 kilometre race with a short inverted aerofoil mounted over its cockpit. It was astonishingly quick. Overshadowed, the Porsche factory team objected that the aerofoil blocked the view of following drivers and the organisers requested that it be removed. The Mays tried again at Monza where the scrutineers did not like the look of it and it was rejected outright. The Mays gave up the experiment in despair.

At this time the function of the Mays' wing was not widely understood, though the theory behind it was simple enough. They saw that loading a car's tyres so that they are pressed harder to the track surface increases adhesion and thus the car can corner faster, can brake within a shorter distance and can accelerate with less tendency towards wheelspin. However, it was a widely held view that a co-efficient of friction of unity could not physically be exceeded, consequently a car could not in any event corner at a force exceeding 1.0g.

Making a car heavier increases the loading on its tyres but that is no way to enhance cornering power since, in effect the additional mass multiplies the centrifugal force trying to make the car fly off into the bushes. Its inertia also makes acceleration slower and increases braking distances. On the contrary, lighter is faster. However, May saw no reason why aerodynamic downforce - negative lift - should not be employed to load the tyres without increasing the inertia weight of the machine.

The spoiler invented by Ginther was intended to counter unwanted lift rather than to harness a significant amount of download. However, the early Sixties found Michael May working at Maranello as a consultant employed to help develop fuel injection. He advised on development of the 250P's so called "aerodynamic roll bar". This was a wide roll hoop at the back of the open cockpit matching windscreen height and carefully shaped to deflect air down towards the spoiler. Although it echoed the May Porsche's wing, then Ferrari Technical Director Mauro Forghieri emphasised to the author that its primary role was as a feed to the spoiler.

At this stage Ferrari did a certain amount of wind tunnel testing, the main aim of the programme to reduce drag. None of the early Sixties racing car manufacturers made any attempt to harness a significant amount of downforce. Indeed, although at this time tyre improvements were starting to challenge the force of gravity, few suspected that aerodynamic downforce could help unlock cornering forces that would allow a car to defy gravity as blatantly as a motorcyclist on a Wall of Death.

Low drag was the universal creed. Ferrari was careful to mitigate positive lift at the rear by means of the spoiler so as to keep its cars driveable. Other than that, it was concerned to minimise drag. Lift spoils drag. Whether positive or negative, any magnitude of lift brings an unavoidable drag penalty. May's winged spyder had been intended to trade that loss for enhanced adhesion: it was not an exchange to which Ferrari or others gave serious consideration at this time.

Indeed, few early Sixties racing car engineers were more than superficially concerned with aerodynamic form. In Formula One wheels had to be exposed and conventional wisdom was to make the fuselage as low and slim as possible. Formula One cars were not generally wind tunnel tested, were logically cigar shaped and their constructors concentrated upon the reduction of frontal area. Bodywork was shaped to look right and keep tight. The huge front engined Vanwall had been the last significant Grand Prix car to put co-efficient of drag as a matter of the highest priority.

Having enclosed wheels and a greater expanse of bodywork, sports-racing cars had to pay much more attention to the co-efficient of drag. Clearly, with a high windscreen mandatory, the frontal area was predetermined: the drag co-efficient was not. However, few constructors other than Ferrari had access to wind tunnel test facilities. In the early Sixties, few sought access. By and large both productionised Gran Turismo racers and one-off Experimental GTs were streamlined according to art and intuition rather than science. The shapes adopted were those which looked right.

1963 found Ford of Detroit working on a design study for an Experimental GT car with a mid engine and a fully enclosed coupe body. Ford designers started with a mid engined roadster version of the production Mustang and ended up with a shape not dissimilar to that of the Lola GT. Wind tunnel tests revealed at a simulated 200m.p.h. drag of around 500lbs. (225kg.) traded for front axle lift of a similar magnitude and rear axle lift one third that of the front.

In conventional fashion, the initial Ford nose shape resembled the prow of a barge. Lowering the bonnet line and fitting a bib spoiler under the radiator air intake while ducting the heated air out through the top of the bonnet proved a beneficial modification. It marginally reduced drag - probably through discouraging air from

flowing under the car, where a ground shear effect adds drag - while cutting front axle lift by almost 50%, albeit significantly increasing lift at the other end of the car.

The magnitude of positive lift Ford ended up with was considered manageable, the drag was a low as Ford had dared hope for. The car now resembled even more closely the overall shape of the Lola GT and with Ford having commissioned its production of Broadley rather than Ford Indy Car builder Chapman it was even fitted with Lola-copy doors.

In 1963, the Lola GT raced at Silverstone, the Nurburgring and Le Mans without distinction, then became a test bed for Ford parts. Ford had its own ideas on chassis technology, though its agreement with Lola made Broadley responsible for the design of everything under that low drag g.r.p. shell shaped by Detroit styling.

Alas, Broadley found himself without the design freedom he had originally been promised and the idea of an advanced aluminium and steel monocoque gave way to a heavy steel fabrication under pressure from Detroit. The main problem was that there was confusion at Detroit as to the ultimate purpose of the car. It had started out as an exercise specifically to win Le Mans but soon there were those who wanted it to be a real production GT car rather than a pure racer. As Broadley recalled in an interview with Motor Sport:

"I said, look, if you are going to build a race car, build a race car, don't try to turn this thing into a semi-production car. It's not raceable. It ended up with a head to head with one particular guy, and I couldn't see the point of continuing. The infiltration had got to a point where it had clearly gone wrong, and I wasn't prepared to put up with that. It was basically my fault for not holding the situation together in the first place. In retrospect it would have been very difficult to do but I should have done it".

Broadley took Lola out of the project again in 1964, the year the so called GT40 (after its 40 inch height) made a premature debut at Le Mans. It was really a committee-designed car, the way it ended up. It had a monocoque reminiscent of the Lola GT but full length and with more lateral bracing in the centre. Produced from substantial sheet steel, the tub was very stiff but was also of considerable weight. In general terms the running gear followed the pattern of the Lola with a similar powertrain. However, throughout it was clean sheet of paper design rather than a revised version of the Mk.VI.

At Le Mans in '63 the Lola had been undergeared and hadn't managed to exceed 150m.p.h. on the long, three and a half mile Mulsanne straight. Ford was looking for an honest 200m.p.h. but at the Le Mans practice in April the new car proved unstable at speeds in excess of 100m.p.h. It was not clear if this was an aerodynamic fault or a suspension development problem. Ford's key engineer took the view that it was a suspension fault and toyed with rear suspension adjustments.

To no avail. The prototype crashed heavily at the Mulsanne kink, its driver lucky to escape with his life. The second prototype was then taken to the British MIRA testing ground where the test drivers sensed the tail of the car lift and adopt a corkscrew-like motion at high speed, the effect reminiscent of an arrow without feathers. The problem, hence its solution was aerodynamic. A three inch high rear deck spoiler made the car stable to the extent that it could be driven at 170m.p.h. with hands off the steering wheel.

Subsequent investigation in the full sized MIRA wind tunnel showed the basic design creating 313lb. lift at the rear wheels at 200mp.h. - far more than the Ford's model tests had suggested. With the spoiler increased in height to 4.5 inches negative lift was apparent, to the extent of 132lb. and for no increase in drag.

A tail spoiler does not automatically increase drag since by pressurising the air close to the deck it helps it stay attached: it is when the boundary layer air breaks away and becomes turbulent rather than a smooth laminer flow that drag is induced. The earlier the break-away, the greater the drag. Ford found a taller, 6.0 inch spoiler created 192lb. downforce but drag had then started to rise. The 4.5 inch spoiler was standardised and with it the drag co-efficient was allegedly in the region of Cd Ç 0.35.

For the Le Mans race Ford rush-prepared three GT40s which lined up against an armada of six 3.2 and 4.0 litre V12 Ferraris in what was now called the GT Prototype class. Ferrari's models were known, respectively, as the 275P

and the 330P, both versions utilising the familiar '63 chassis with its open cockpit and aerodynamic roll bar. On the first lap Ginther's GT40 trailed three of the red cars but on the second lap he passed all of them on the Mulsanne, exceeding 200m.p.h. in the process. The Ford - Ferrari battle was on in earnest.

Understandably, Ford did not win the Le Mans marathon until its third attempt. By 1966 it had long dropped any pretence of racing a prototype of a GT car, although such a philosophy had been in the spirit of the GT Prototype nee Experimental GT class. The GT Prototype class had now given way to a new 'Group 6' category in recognition of the fact that in '65 and '66 Ford and Ferrari were both fielding pure mid engined racing cars.

The term Sports-Prototype was coined. The Sports-Prototype was, of course, truly a prototype of nothing in the way of a practical sports car, and it was far removed from the concept of a Gran Turismo. There was no confusion about its purpose, though. A glorious beast with bags of power and a beautiful shape, it was a breed of pure, uncompromised long distance racing machine every bit as stimulating as the Formula One sprint car.

Group 6 regulations imposed no capacity limit on this new animal and did not pretend to do much more than ensure that it sported a proper windscreen and had lights, a spare tyre and nominal luggage space, in the general spirit of sports car racing. There was, however, a minimum weight limit of 800kg. for large displacement cars while there were certain dimensional criteria, such as restrictions on overhang. However, it was now permitted for the windscreen to be narrower than the body.

Ferrari took advantage of that potential for reduced frontal area with its mid Sixties Sports-Prototypes. Further, by '66, in the quest for maximum speed on the Mulsanne, it had started exploiting a fully enclosed coupe body at Le Mans. However, it still produced a version without out a roof panel and with a low horizontal engine cover surmounted by a wide aerodynamic roll bar. Ferrari's quasi-spyder saved weight and allowed further development of the aerodynamic roll bar concept, though significant downforce had not yet entered the performance equation.

In 1966 low drag was still everything. The contemporary Ferrari Sports-Prototype did not have a full width windscreen, the Ford GT40 did. Thus the Ford's frontal area was significantly higher, hence total drag was high in spite of a good drag co-efficient. The '66 Le Mans winning Ford Mk.II was also unsubtle in the engine department. It had retained the GT40 chassis, equipping it with a pushrod V8 engine from the world of Stock Car racing which boasted an sledgehammer 7.0 litre displacement.

The rival Ferrari P2 and P3 models utilised a more sophisticated twin overhead camshaft, 24 valve alloy V12 displacing 4.0 litres, the latest version having fuel injection. Ford ran its simple, old fashioned but dependable wedge head engine to just over 6000r.p.m while Ferrari's better breathing, better burning hemi head unit peaked at 8,000r.p.m. and produced more power per revolution. In Ford's case power came out at something the region of 485b.h.p. - say 11.0b.h.p. per litre per 1000r.p.m. - in Ferrari's case, at approximately 420b.h.p. - 13.0b.h.p. per litre per 1000r.p.m.

The only other player in this high power heavyweight contest arrived in 1966: the Chevrolet-Chaparral 2D. This was another all-American car, one based on a g.r.p. monocoque, albeit with aluminium reinforcement and steel bulkheads to carry the suspension. Born in the early Sixties, the unconventional Chaparral chassis had conventional running gear aside from its clutchless transmission and was equipped with a pushrod, wedge head V8 engine displacing 5.36 litres. The so called Small Block Chevrolet was familiar in American motorsport circles and in this guise it produced around 450b.h.p. at 6,500r.p.m. - a commendable 13.0b.h.p. per litre per 1000r.p.m.

The unconventional transmission was a clue to the Chaparral's special link with Chevrolet. It was an experimental two speed only unit developed by GM's Tech Centre at Warren near Detroit. Jim Hall's Chaparral team had forged a very special relationship with the Tech Centre, to the extent that had become virtually a back door Chevrolet racing team. It had started out contesting purely domestic races, utilising a low windscreen spyder body. In this guise the Chaparral, which first ran in 1963, took constructor Hall to victory in the 1965 United States Road Racing Championship (U.S.R.R.C.), and in the Sebring 12 Hours, the latter a Formula Libre event won against the Ford and Ferrari Group 6 coupes.

Over the years '63 - '65 the Chaparral spyder first acquired a nose air dam to rid the original tendency for its front end to lift at speed, then this was replaced by an entirely new, cleaner nose profile that did the job without the same sensitivity to pitch. In the meantime, a rear spoiler had sprouted to keep the tail as firmly checked as the front end. Further developments included tabs on the front wings ahead of the wheel arches and hot air ducting through the top of the nose section, GT40-style. In 1965 louvers were set into the top of each front wheel air to bleed off the high pressure caused by wheel rotation.

The bibs and louvers disappeared when the spyder body was fitted with a hardtop - forming a conventional coupe shape - for 1966 International races. It was a much cleaner car that travelled to Europe for the Nurburgring 1000km. and Le Mans 24 Hour classics. The Chaparral won at the 'Ring but retired from Le Mans.

Back home, the spyder version of the Chevrolet-Chaparral had adopted an aluminium monocoque and in 1966 was entered for the first so called 'Can Am' series in radical 2E guise. This series was an extension of the existing fierce North American competition for unlimited capacity 'Group 7', or free-design one-off sports cars. The only important chassis dictates were for enclosed wheels and a spare wheel on board. Weight was free.

Since Group 7 competition was sprint-race based, the regulations were an invitation to cram a huge engine into the smallest, lightest possible sports-racing chassis. That thinking had been responsible for the Chaparral's unusual g.r.p. tub. The Small Block Chevrolet, a 4.7 litre version of the Ford Fairlane V8 and a similar displacement Oldsmobile V8 were typical of favoured '65 engines. Running on high octane American racing fuel over short distances, these pushrod V8s could produce over twice the output of a contemporary 1.5 litre Formula One engine.

In 1964 Cooper Grand Prix driver Bruce McLaren had produced his own semi-monocoque Group 7 spyder propelled by an Oldsmobile V8. The Elva company had come to an agreement to manufacture customer replicas of the McLaren chassis for 1965, and these were equipped with a variety of engines, many examples crossing the Atlantic. In the mid Sixties Group 7 racing was becoming popular among privateers on both sides of the pond and Elva sold 15 chassis in '65. Meanwhile, McLaren had produced an updated works car to take the fight to Chaparral and a new rival: Lola.

Having left the GT40 project Broadley had revived his own marque with spaceframe then monocoque single seaters. The spaceframe cars were Formula Two machines derived from the Mk.V and were known as Types 54 and 55 while the '65 monocoque was the Type 60. The Type 70 was a 1965 Group 7 sports-racer, Broadley having seen the same lucrative customer market that Elva had spotted.

The Lola T70 was a monocoque spyder designed to accept any chosen American V8 engine. Its monocoque tub was full length like the GT40 but was much lighter since it was produced from a mixture of steel and aluminium alloy. Throughout there was a steel framework to which aluminium panels were spot welded while the torsion boxes comprised aluminium fuel tanks produced by Abbey Panels which were hung from steel inner walls, rigidly attached via flanges top and bottom. A total capacity of 32 gallons was provided for by the twin D-section tanks. At the front, the box section steel framework was in part double skinned in aluminium then foam filled for additional rigidity. All suspension pick ups were steel fabrications.

The pedal box area was fully enclosed and the aluminium floor ran back as far as the firewall bulkhead which was of triangular longitudinal section, the slope forming the seat back. The engine was bolted in as a semi-stressed member of the assembly, the tub extending back to a hoop-style rear bulkhead embracing the transmission. Ahead of the pedal box, twin radiators and the spare wheel were carried by the g.r.p. nose, though after the first six chassis an aluminium box was provided to carry the radiators,

since the nose could then be made readily detachable via pip-pins.

The spyder body was a very low, very sleek production by Peter Jackson's Specialist Mouldings concern, which had manufactured the original GT40 body and earlier plastic shell Lolas. It incorporated nose top ducting for the radiators and a low-lying perspex windscreen. The flat centre section of the g.r.p. body (with the cockpit opening) was bolted in place and extended downwards to wrap around the curved flanks of the side tanks, while the g.r.p. tail into which it blended was quickly-detachable. The nose incorporated an undertray but the floor of the engine bay was left open in the interest of cooling.

The help keep it light, the T70 spyder was of modest length, its wheelbase comparable to that of the 1.5 litre Formula One Lola and the GT40 and a little longer than that of the Mk.VI, which was in the interest of stability. The most unusual aspect of the running gear was the fact that the brake discs were mounted inboard of the 15" wheel rims to get the best possible cooling flow. In the face of rising car performance disc temperature management for consistent operation and adequate pad wear had become a major challenge. The inboard discs encroached upon space where suspension linkages would otherwise have run and the arrangement was thus a key suspension design influence.

The solid cast iron discs were Girling productions, as were their single pot calipers which were equipped with Ferodo DS11 pads. At the rear the disc was inboard of the upright, sandwiched between a flange on the inner end of the hub and a flange on the outer end of the driveshaft. The magnesium upright was taller than the disc so that wishbone linkages could pick up both top and bottom.

The discs were formed with an integral bell and at the front the bell was pronounced so that a short upright could sit within it. The lower wishbone then picked up on the middle of the upright, only just below hub level. A steel stub axle was carried by the magnesium upright and the lower wishbone pick up was almost diametrically opposed to it, stepped down a little and attached to the same flange that bolted into the upright. The hub ran on taper roller bearings on

14

the stub axle and had six studs which passed through the disc then the wheel.

The front suspension was via unequal and non-parallel wishbones and outboard spring/damper units, the wishbones two-piece. The lower wishbone took the form of a substantial main leg and slender brake reaction strut with a cup formed in the main leg housing the lower spring/damper attachment. The rear suspension was likewise via wishbones and outboard spring/damper units, with the wishbones reversed and radius arms running forward to the firewall bulkhead. Front and rear, steel coils were fitted over Armstrong oil dampers.

The transmission incorporated the new LG500 Hewland gearbox, which offered a lightweight magnesium gearbox case cum c.w.p. carrier which was bolted to Lola's own magnesium bellhousing. The longitudinal, outboard two shaft, non-synchromesh four speeder was fed by a Scheifer single plate coil spring (rather than diaphragm) clutch.

Lola had been the first customer for the original Hewland production racing car gearbox, a Formula Junior unit introduced in 1960 and based on a VW casing and retaining a VW c.w.p. and differential. Later came the all-Hewland HD four and five speed units used in 1.5 litre Formula One cars and larger capacity sports cars, up to 3.5 litres. The Hewland HD had a lightweight magnesium case and was non-synchromesh to save weight and speed shifts while having constant mesh straight cut gears running on caged needle roller bearings on the input and output shafts, the former passing forward from the clutch under the c.w.p, the latter being the pinion shaft.

A major feature of the Hewland gearbox was that its dog-clutch engaged gear ratios could be altered at the circuit with access to the gears provided via a detachable end cover. The main case incorporated the c.w.p. housing and was bolted to an appropriate bellhousing for the given engine. In 1964 Hewland anticipated the growth of Group 7 racing and designed the LG500 four speed for use with large capacity American V8 engines, the first example finding its way into the prototype T70 spyder. In essence, the LG was a beefed-up version of the HD and it employed Hewland's own differential.

Lubrication was again via splash while weight was 136lb.

John Surtees, rival to McLaren in Formula One, had set up his own team to campaign the LG500 equipped T70 as a semi-works effort in '65. He tested the first car with a 4.5 litre Oldsmobile engine, then switched to a 5.0 litre Small Block Chevrolet, mid season to a 5.9 litre version of the same. Traco fettled these potent wet sump, carburettor-equipped V8s, the big Chevrolet capable of over 550b.h.p. on high octane fuel. Early T70 customers included Harald Young Racing - for British events with a 4.7 litre Ford V8 - and Lola's North American concessionaire John Mecom - two examples with similar engines for the U.S.R.R.C. By the end of the '65 season, two more chassis had been sold to British customers, eight more to American customers, total output matching that of Elva.

Meanwhile, Broadley had evolved a Mk.II version, the aim to further reduce weight and take advantage of the fact that a spare wheel would not have to be carried under '66 regulations. Since the spare wheel had been carried in the nose, this was revised, lighter and sleeker with better radiator ventilation. The twin radiators were replaced by a single unit.

The tub was revised, a little stiffer and a little lighter. The rear bulkhead stood proud of the rear legs and a triangular bracing member was introduced at this junction while some other areas were likewise stiffened in the light of experience. More importantly, the aluminium fuel tanks were replaced by aircraft-style bags, thus the torsion box assemblies could be lighter without loss of rigidity. Further, there had been a problem of fuel leakage in view of the torsional loading imposed upon the fully stressed alloy tanks.

The rear suspension geometry was revised, the lower radius rod pick ups on the firewall bulkhead moving inwards to sit immediately ahead of the chassis pick ups for the lower wishbones. The upper radius arm pick ups were moved inward to a lesser extent. Handling was thus improved while braking performance was enhanced via the introduction of radially ventilated discs, these attached to a separate aluminium bell.

Team Surtees had race-tested the T70 Mk.II

in '65, the new car immediately proving much quicker than the original. Surtees won the Guards International Trophy at Brands Hatch over McLaren but at the equally prestigious Pepsi 100 supporting the Canadian Grand Prix on the Mosport Park circuit a suspension failure pitched him off the track. The prototype Mk.II was written off in a huge accident, Surtees was lucky to escape with his life. It put him out for the remainder of the season. A season in which the T70 took a total of six wins, putting Lola in the forefront of international Group 7 racing.

With the Can Am series in 1966 Group 7 came of age. The Can Am was big money and that allied to the sheer spectacle of the cars attracted huge interest. It was a battle of three marques, Lola, McLaren and Chaparral, over six races, four in the USA, two in Canada. Surtees won half the races and emerged overall victor in the factory supported Small Block-Mk.II T70 and in so doing won more money than had been on offer for winning all the World Championship Grand Prix races that year.

The Small Block Chevrolet was the engine of the year, McLaren having to switch from the smaller capacity if lighter Oldsmobile unit to stay competitive. The Mk.II version of the T70 was reckoned to be the best handling customer Can Am car while the Chaparral 2E - still a works-only project - was the most radical. The Chaparral continued to show its GM ties with the introduction of a special lightweight aluminium block. Aside from its equally special transmission, it came out with a very important new aerodynamic tweak.

The '66 2E Can Am Chaparral re-invented the wing. Where May had placed a large wing over the cockpit of his spyder to act through the centre of gravity, Hall set his wing higher up and over the tail, to act directly through the rear suspension uprights. To overcome the problem of the additional drag created by the wing, Hall arranged for a hydraulic tipping system, whereby pressure on a foot pedal would trim the wing to its minimum drag, minimum downforce position. Thus the driver would keep his foot on the wing pedal on the straight, releasing it under braking for additional drag as well as its downthrust. Many saw the high post mounted device as a means of aiding braking and stabil-

ity, overlooking its key role as a means of enhancing grip.

Having proven the wing in Can Am, Chaparral planned a '67 Group 6 endurance car using the device. Meanwhile, Broadley was hatching his own Sports-Prototype - essentially a coupe bodied version of the T70 spyder. Various parties had expressed an interest in an endurance racing spin-off from the popular Can Am Lola. Broadley saw that a model derived from the T70 should be able to be homologated into the Group 4 category for 50-off machines. Including '67 Mk.II production, Lola had built 47 examples of the T70.

Group 4 was intended to give privateers a goal to aim for. In 1966 it was contested by two cars: the original Fairlane engined Ford GT40 with a 4.7 litre displacement and the 3.3 litre V12 Ferrari 250LM. Neither of these privately campaigned machines could muster much more than 350b.h.p. A Small Block Chevrolet engined T70 coupe would leave them breathless. Further, it could be a straightforward conversion of the spyder chassis allowing customers to switch between Can Am and endurance racing using the same mechanical base.

A Sports-Prototype chassis would also suit Aston Martin, since the marque was looking to take its brand new V8 engine to Le Mans. It had already used a Mk.II development car for a test of its 5.0 litre unit in the summer of '66. Aston Martin had supplied Lola with an experimental Weber carburettor equipped wet sump engine, of which the sump had been far too deep. It had therefore been necessary to cut and lower the sump to fit the engine into the car, which at the same time evaluated the first Hewland DG gearbox.

The car was immediately very quick, clocking an 87 second lap of Silverstone. Alas, after only a handful of tours it rolled into the pits making loud clanking noises. There was a lack of oil pressure and a further exploratory lap was undertaken, only for a rod to come through the side of the block. The clanking noise had told of a broken big end cap!

Undaunted by this experience, and by a subsequent test at Goodwood that ended in another con rod failure, Aston Martin was keen for Surtees to take its challenge to Le Mans in 1967.

The coupe version of the Lola T70 was born in 1967 and flourished through to the end of the decade, prior to the rise of the Porsche 917 and Ferrari 512, both of which enjoyed more sophisticated engine technology. The colour photographs on the following eight pages show, in order, Epstein/ Liddell at Francorchamps in '68 (left), the start of the same year's Sebring 12 Hour race with de Udy leading midfield runners, the Charlton/Fisher car at the following month's Brands Hatch bout, the Penske Mk.IIIB of 1969 at Daytona and the Brabham/ Hulme Mk.III at Brands Hatch in 1967.

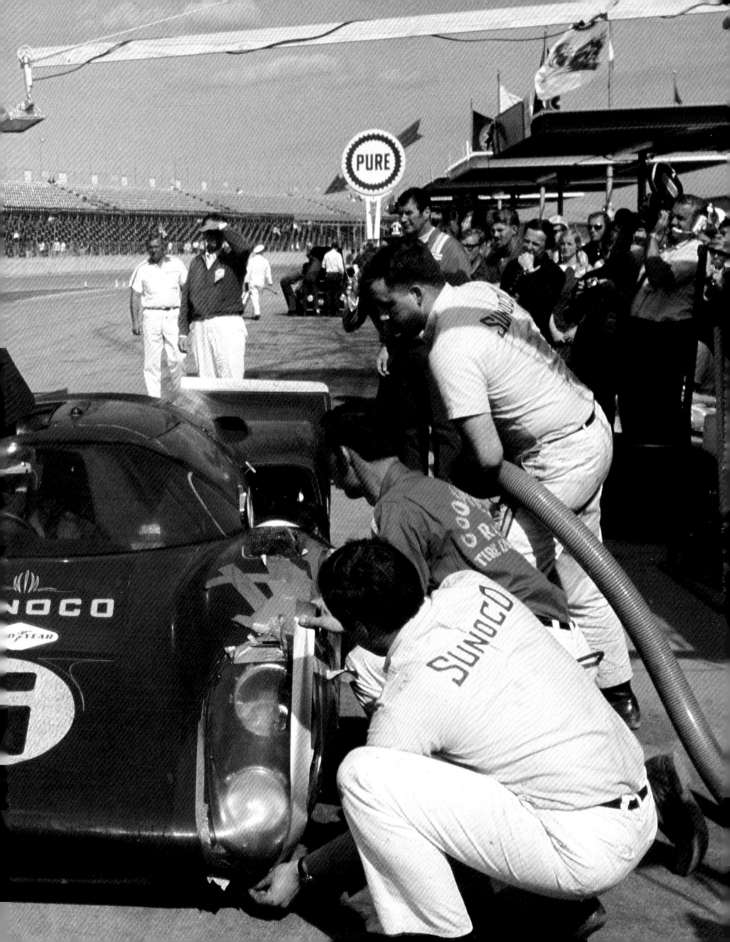

False Start

Lola's splendid '66 Can Am Championship success with Surtees followed a superb Indianapolis 500 win for Graham Hill in the T90: the company rode into '67 on the crest of a wave. It was once again to produce a Grand Prix car, Surtees having joined Honda's effort and found the Japanese challenger powerful but in need of a new chassis. This would be based on the T90, though heavily adapted to the requirements of the Honda Racing project run by Team Surtees from its Slough base. In addition, there were more Indy Cars to build, and a Formula Two chassis for BMW aside from a large batch of T70s in familiar spyder and new Mk.III Coupe form.

With so much money on offer in Can Am, and with the T70 the Champion car, demand for the spyder was greater than ever from wealthy amateur racers. Business was brisk for 38 year old Eric Broadley's Lola Cars Ltd. concern. Broadley oversaw design work but had a four-strong team of design draughtsmen at his Slough base. Testing of 25% models in a fixed floor wind tunnel was part of the design process. The cars were produced at Slough with casting work sub contracted, machining and fabrication in house and g.r.p. bodywork supplied by Specialised Mouldings. The chassis plate designation 'SL' to be found on '67 Lolas indicated Slough built as opposed to the earlier Bromley built family.

The new T70 Coupe was attractive to the privateer in view of its anticipated Group 4 homologation in Chevrolet guise and Lola bought a batch of 460b.h.p.-rated 5.5 litre (333cu.in.) Ryan Falconer-fettled V8s which were fitted as standard. However, customers could specify alternative pushrod V8 engines while the so called 'T73' version was produced to accept the overhead-cam Aston Martin engine.

Surtees had now set up Lola Racing Ltd. which was jointly owned by Team Surtees and Lola and was managed by Howard Marsden, formerly of Alan Mann Racing. Its aim was to act as a works team for Lola, running BMW and Cosworth engined T100 Formula Two cars as well as Aston Martin (Coupe) and Chevrolet (spyder) engined T70s.

The Aston Martin effort was run by Cyril Audrey. Mexican Pedro Rodriguez and young Englishmen Chris Irwin and David Hobbs signed for Lola Racing, of which 1964 World Champion Surtees was, of course, to be lead driver. Rodriguez (brother of the late Riccardo) had a Cooper Formula One contract for 1967. Formula Three star Irwin had made his Grand Prix debut in '66 at Brands Hatch but had yet to find a regular Formula One drive, while Hobbs was similarly aspiring to move up, having made his mark in Formula Two.

In '66 Hobbs had regularly campaigned a private Ferrari 250LM and he had won the final non-championship sportscar race of the season at Roy Hesketh in South Africa, sharing a GT40. A week later Rodriguez won the opening round of the '67 World Championship, the South African Grand Prix at Kyalami. Then the World Championship for Manufacturers opened in North America with a 24 Hour race at Daytona in early February, which was followed by a 12 Hour race at Sebring on April 1.

In the Daytona Continental Ferrari trounced Ford and Chevrolet-Chaparral, Rodriguez sharing the third placed NART entered P3 which finished behind two of the new factory P4s. Ford ran six of its Mk.IIs but only one finished, in a lowly seventh place. The latest winged Chaparral 2F had a 7.0 litre 'Big Block' Chevrolet engine and set fastest lap but crashed while a sister 2D was another retirement. At Sebring Ford debuted its latest honeycomb chassis Mk.IV in the absence of Ferrari. It battled the 2F, which again set fastest lap but retired, as did the sister 2D once more. The one other works car, a Ford Mk.II finished a delayed second.

At Sebring a privately entered Small Block T70 Mk.III Coupe ran in the hands of Buck Fulp and Roger McClusky as a Group 6 machine, Group 4 homologation not yet confirmed. It arrived late, its suspension was damaged in practice and it did not race. A false start, then, for the T70 as a Sports-Prototype. A week later came the Le Mans test days and the first public outing for the Firestone shod Aston Martin-Lola. This factory supported effort was not intended to challenge for the World Championship, but carried Aston Martin's renewed hopes at La Sarthe some eight years after the marque's Le Mans triumph with the DBR1.

However, although Aston Martin ambitiously planned to field three cars, it was operating on a very small budget compared to Ford. Ford had taken three years and millions of dollars to find success, a success it was equally determined to repeat this year. Running an unproven engine, Aston Martin had neither time nor money on its side.

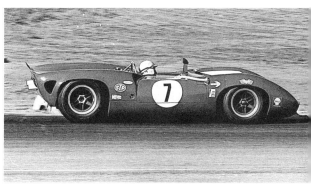

Flashback to '66 - the previous year's performance of the spyder version of the T70 justified Lola's "world beater" tag, John Surtees (middle picture) winning the Can Am Championship. Also pictured are fellow Grand Prix drivers Graham Hill (lower picture) assisting Surtees' Can Am effort and Denny Hulme driving Sid Taylor's Mk.I spyder in a '66 British Group 7 race.

Gran Turismo

DP218 V-8
90 degree V8
98.0 x 83.0mm./5005.99cc.
Unblown
Aluminium alloy block and heads
Wet cast iron liners
5 main bearings, plain
Steel crankshaft, 4 pins
Steel con rods
Brico light alloy pistons
AE rings
D.o.h.c, chain driven
2 valves/cylinder, 1 plug
66 degree included valve angle
Scintilla ignition
4 Weber carburettors
Compression ratio 11:1
238 kg.

Aston Martin originally intended its V8 engine for its Experimental GT racing programme of the early Sixties. The marque's sturdy straight six engine had clearly been reaching the limit of its development potential and the V8 replacement road engine was coming on stream. As ever, Aston Martin was keen to develop the new engine through racing. The V8 was intended to supply a Gran Turismo with in excess of 300b.h.p. and as 65b.h.p. per litre could be expected from a road engine it was designed for a displacement of around 5.0 litres.

Work had commenced in 1961 under Tadek Marek. Marek was a Polish engineer and driver - he won the 1939 Polish Grand Prix - who had been head-hunted from the British Motor Corporation in 1955 by John Wyer, then recently appointed Technical Director of Aston Martin. Wyer had straightaway re-organised Aston Martin engineering, setting up a proper race shop and putting Marek in charge of road car engine design.

At that stage, Marek had undertaken the task of drawing up the straight six on the basis that it would have an iron block since that was where all his experience lay. Further, he stipulated it should not be raced since he had no experience of designing a racing engine. The first stipulation went out of the window at the production stage since in 1956 Aston Martin could find a foundry with surplus capacity for aluminium work but not one with room for iron casting.

Of course, the use of aluminium meant that the engine had greater potential for competition work. The straight six displaced 3670cc. and when in 1957 Le Mans dropped its 3.0 litre capacity limit Wyer jumped at the chance to use it. The one example he tried failed and the 3.0 litre limit was back in '58. However, enlarged to 4160cc. Marek's six propelled the Project 212

Experimental GT of '62 and the Project 214 of '63, the V8 running late.

The 90 degree V8 initially had the cylinder dimensions and proven combustion chamber design and valve gear of the two valve, twin cam, hemi head straight six. Right from the outset this model was aluminium alloy, though carrying wet cast iron liners. Known as Project DP215, it was shelved at the end of the '63 season when the marque shut down its Experimental and Racing Departments in a cost cutting exercise, only to be revived a year or so later. The Project was then coded DP218.

Given the straight six cylinder dimensions, the capacity was 4803.75cc. (96mm. x 83mm.) and bench tests commenced in the summer of '65, development taking power from an early 275b.h.p. at 5,750r.p.m. to 325b.h.p. at 6,200r.p.m. the compression ratio increasing from 8.4:1 to 9.0:1. Thus, the output of the road going six had been comfortably exceeded and Aston Martin had the power level it wanted for its new generation Gran Turismo roadster.

In '66 work commenced on an experimental racing version of the V8, this having a 97.5mm. bore, hence displacing 4955.0cc. It was equipped with four Weber 48IDAs and had a compression ratio of 11.0:1. On Le Mans regulation 100 octane fuel it was coaxed to give 421b.h.p. at a modest 6,500r.p.m. this representing 13.1b.h.p. per litre per 1000r.p.m with torque of 386lb.ft. at 5,000r.p.m. This was the engine tested in a T70 Can Am chassis at Silverstone in the summer of '66.

Since the DP218 engine was designed for road use it was based on a two plane - 90 degree phased - rather than single plane - 180 degree phased - crankshaft. The single plane crankshaft V8 operates as two four cylinder engines, each bank running separately to the benefit of exhaust tuning potential on the interference principle. It is possible to blend pipes from opposite banks when a two plane shaft is run, but this creates car installation difficulties. Aston Martin did not resort to a cross-over exhaust system.

On the other hand, the advantage of the two plane 'shaft is smoother running: in this form a V8 is properly balanced, whereas the flat plane crank causes a secondary out of balance which manifests itself as a side to side shake of the 'shaft. The smooth running nature of the two

plane crankshaft 90 degree V8 is a distinct advantage for endurance running.

The racing version of the V8 was not planned to be highly stressed in the light of its intended Le Mans 24 hour programme, Aston Martin designing it from the outset for a maximum engine speed of only 6,750r.p.m. That speed was very modest for a 626cc. cylinder given a stroke:bore ratio of 0.847 and the major concern was not the level of piston speed or piston acceleration but was controlling the large diameter - hence weighty - valves which enabled the unit to breathe well. The valves were driven directly, through inverted bucket tappets, this following long standing Coventry Climax racing engine practice.

The new engine was very compact given its sizeable displacement. The basis of DP218 was an alloy monobloc that extended well below the crankshaft centreline for bottom end rigidity. In further pursuit of that goal, the crankcase was well ribbed and gussetted while the sump cum lower crankcase was formed of alloy. As we have noted, the wet sump was rather deep, requiring modification by Lola. Five main bearings were employed, with steel bearing caps. The liners were top seated and were free to expand at the lower end, this arrangement avoiding problems of the differential in the expansion of alloy and iron.

The crankshaft was nitrided steel, running in plain bearings and having a main bearing journal diameter of 2.75 ins. It was driven by semi slipper-type pistons through I-section steel con rods, those pistons equipped with two compression and one oil control ring, the latter of the three-piece type. The pistons had a slightly stepped crown. The light alloy heads carried single plugs, austenitic iron valve seat inserts and alloy bronze valve guides. The twin camshafts were driven via a Duplex chain system on the front end.

Also on the front end was a belt drive system for the water pump and the oil pump. Ignition was via a Scintilla magneto, this initially mounted at the front of the righthand bank and driven via a skew gear of the front of the exhaust camshaft. For installation reasons, in the T70 coupe the old fashioned magneto was run off the back of the gearbox via a belt.

Induction was via downdraught porting emerging in the centre of the vee, each bank served by a pair of downdraught 48IDA twin choke Weber carburettors, though fuel injection was envisaged. Injection promised accurate fuelling throughout the engine's working speed range.

The downdraught carburettor arrangement made for a complex throttle linkage. Tall trumpets topped the induction system while each bank's independent exhaust system blended four long primary pipes into a single megaphone tailpipe. The overall length of the unit was 711mm, while its weight was 238kg. - not a great improvement over the thinwall iron block Chevrolet V8 carried in T70 spyders.

The big end failure on the engine in the Silverstone spyder was attributed by Aston Martin to Lola's sump modification, which incorporated a trap door system to stop surge. However, Aston

Martin had experienced some problems with con rod caps in bench testing and the later Goodwood failure emphasised the weakness, which was traced to the lubrication of the big end bearing. The con rods were redesigned for '67 while a dry sump system was introduced. Two scavenge and one pressure pump were mounted on a common shaft, replacing the wet sump pump.

For '67 the capacity was increased further to 5005.99cc. via a 98mm. bore and power was increased to 450b.h.p. at 6,500r.p.m., representing 13.8b.h.p. per litre per 1000r.p.m. with torque of 413lb.ft. at 5000r.p.m. This was the test bench performance of the first engine installed in a coupe chassis. The T73 was shown at the January '67 Racing Car Show on the Team Surtees stand, then ran initially at Snetterton in March '67.

The Aston Martin V8 engine was initially equipped with Weber twin choke carburettors. It is seen here on its first public outing, at the '67 Le Mans test.

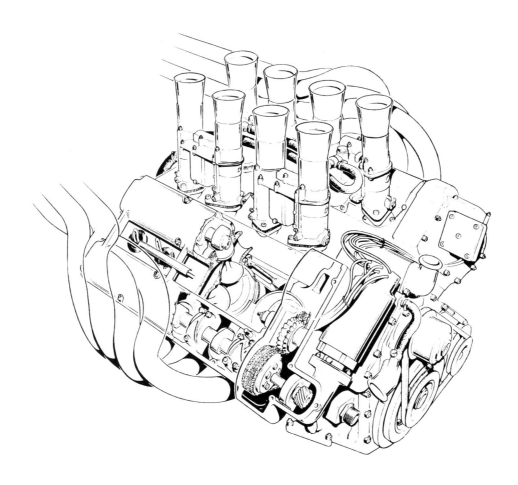

In the Post

90 degree V8
4.04in. (102.6mm.) x 3.25in. (82.6mm.)/ 333 cu. in. (5.46 litres)
Unblown
Iron block, aluminium heads
Linerless
5 main bearings, plain
Steel crankshaft, 4 pins
Steel con rods
Diamond Racing light alloy pistons
Sealed Power rings
Pushrod, chain driven
2 valves/cylinder, 1 plug
Parallel valves
51.9mm. inlet valve, 41.0mm. exhaust
Lucas ignition
4 Weber carburettors
Compression ratio 11:1

Chevrolet introduced its classic pushrod V8 engine in 1955. Supplies were soon plentiful, parts were relatively cheap and the farsighted designers had produced an engine with tremendous development potential. Soon there were many tuners specialising in it, while a huge range of factory and aftermarket performance equipment became available off the shelf. Big port aluminium heads, billet crankshafts, roller cams, dry sump lubrication systems, racing pistons, rings, valves, rods and so on and so on. By the mid Sixties a skilled mechanic could build a Chevrolet V8 race engine using parts from a mail order catalogue.

Indeed, by the mid Sixties the 5.0/6.0 litre (300 - 360cu.in.) Small Block Chevrolet had become an American motor sport institution. An important factor in that was the widespread use in the States of high octane racing fuel. This allowed a high compression ratio, and assisted the durability of the production based unit. Given its unsophisticated method of valve actuation, 8,000r.p.m. was reckoned to be about the absolute limit on engine speed, with 6,000- 7,000r.p.m. the level for circuit racing stamina.

One drawback of the pushrod system is that its heavy and complex valve gear implies a loss of rigidity and additional clearances, both these factors costing precision in the transfer of cam movement to valve stem. Worse, the weight of the pushrod assembly causes significant inertia which has to be overcome before the additional load of opening the valve can commence. Thus, the pushrod system strictly limits the rate at which the valves can be operated, to the detriment of gas flow.

The Chevrolet V8 had semi-downdraught porting and a classic wedge-shaped combustion chamber with offset parallel valves and plenty of squish area. The piston crown was flat as standard but carried wedge when a high compression ratio was employed. Although a hemi head with well designed porting could be made to perform better, the Chevrolet design was proven to breathe and burn reasonably well at the modest speed allowed by the pushrod system. Further, the engine was commendably light, despite its iron base. Careful design of a thinwall linerless block had paid dividends in this respect. It was also compact and its light, compact design was part of its track popularity.

Variations on the original block had appeared over the decade or so of the popular Small Block's working life. Race engine builders looked to the block with the thickest bulkheads and employed steel main bearing caps, these secured by four bolts. Well run in blocks were preferred, these free of inherent stresses. Interestingly, the block material, an iron alloy mix, was unchanged since 1955. And the design was fundamentally unaltered, the original dimensions having been just about right.

Extending from closed deck to crank axis, the 90 degree vee monobloc carried a short, stiff crank in five bearings. Plain bearings were run throughout the engine. As standard the crank was of two plane configuration with extended counterbalance webs, thus the engine was in full primary and secondary balance. However, since it was not possible to take full advantage of exhaust pulses to assist scavenging without a cross-over exhaust system, this was occasionally employed, as was a flat plane crankshaft, though only rarely.

A light alloy flywheel was bolted to the steel crankshaft. Chevrolet produced forged steel shafts in various stroke lengths and often with alternative main bearing journal diameters. The non standard forged shaft option was produced from high carbon 1053 alloy and was often nitrided by the race engine builder for improved durability. A torsional vibration damper was always run at the front of the shaft in view of shaft harmonics.

The stock Chevrolet con rod was of typical I-section but the most popular race engine rod was the H-section steel Carrillo rod. Carrillo rods were forged and machined from 4340 steel blanks and were sometimes used with SPS 35N Multi-phase stainless bolts (two per rod). Invariably the piston was attached by a conventional steel gudgeon pin, retained via standard wire circlips.

Typically the semi-slipper type piston was an aftermarket forging - from the likes of Diamond Racing and TRW - with three rings, these often supplied by Sealed Power, with the top ring moly coated. The wedge heads were attached by 17 studs with a steel shim gasket at the block interface.

Head design and preparation was reckoned to be the key to Small Block Chevrolet performance. The head was often an aluminium aftermarket item rather than the stock iron casting. Generally aluminium heads followed the basic pattern of the stock head and retained the small depression in the chamber roof adjacent to the plug that helped produce the turbulence necessary for good burning. However, sometimes the plug was angled and always the ports were enlarged. The original design left enough 'meat' for larger valves and ports to be provided without causing structural difficulties.

The provision of larger valves caused them to be shrouded by the walls of the standard wedge chamber. This made it necessary to relieve the chamber all around its deepest part, where the valves were located. Aside from a stepped piston, the head would be milled to help restore lost compression. Since this caused a misalignment of the intake ports relative to the manifold flange either the ports were reshaped or a bespoke replacement manifold was fitted.

The single camshaft ran deep in the valley of the block and operated the valves (often titanium) through a conventional system of pushrods and rockers. Valve train inertia being a major consideration, lightweight tubular steel pushrods and machined aluminium rockers were employed, the latter running on needle roller bearings. Roller tip lifters replaced the stock hydraulic items which tended to pump up at speed, and represented additional weight.

The replacement rockers were also of the roller type, their roller tips stopping the tendency of the tip of the rocker to slide across the top of the valve stem a high speed, this causing valve guide wear. Similarly, at the camshaft end rollers reduced cam and lifter wear and allowed less clearance and thus more radical valve timing. Invariably at least two springs valve springs were employed, together with an appropriate titanium retainer.

The high lift race camshaft was chain driven on the stock engine (from the front). Some race engine builders preferred the precision of a gear drive whereas others sought the cushioning effect of a chain, and chain drives were highly developed. So too was the typical wet sump lubrication system which was specially baffled.

Ignition was often via conventional magneto while Stateside the most popular carburettor was a single four barrel item. However, for serious road racing a four downdraught Weber set up was more appropriate. The 48IDA twin choke Weber was thus commonly employed, though some of the larger capacity engines ran with bigger bore 58DCOE sidedraught Webers and a cross-over inlet tract system.

The standard issue 333cu.in. Falconer V8 for the T70 was equipped with 48IDAs on a light alloy manifold. It had ported and polished heads, full race reciprocating gear and valve train (the latter chain driven) and a two plane crankshaft. Nevertheless, the standard exhaust was not of the cross-over type. It was equipped with four bolt steel main bearing caps and had baffled wet sump lubrication. Running a compression ratio of 11.0:1 its output was quoted as 460b.h.p. at 6,200r.p.m. - 85b.h.p. per litre and 13.6b.h.p. per litre per 1000 r.p.m.

The latter figure sounds optimistic given the use of 100 octane fuel, though in view of the modest quoted peak power engine speed it was clear that 450b.h.p. was comfortably within reach for a Chevrolet customer. Indeed, for sprint racing, 500b.h.p. might be expected from a long stroke version having the maximum practical displacement of 360cu.in. (5.9 litres) and running to 6,750r.p.m, more in the case of a similar Can Am engine thriving on high octane American racing fuel.

The Revolution

Lola Cars aluminium and steel monocoque
Semi-stressed engine
Outboard front and rear suspension
Koni dampers
Lola magnesium 15" rims
Kelsey Hayes 12.5" diameter cast iron discs, outboard
Kelsey Hayes four pot calipers, Ferodo pads
G.r.p. bodywork
1 Serck water radiator, 2 Serck oil radiators
AP 7 1/4" triple plate clutch
Hewland 5 speed gearbox, Salisbury l.s.d.
145 litre fuel tank, 14 litre oil tank
Varley battery, Smiths instruments
2489mm. wheelbase, 1397mm. front and rear track
820kg.

"The new 200m.p.h. plus Lola Type 70 Mk. III G.T. racing car is the latest in a line of high performance sports and G.T. cars from the drawing board of Eric Broadley.

"A unique feature of this car is that its chassis is identical to that of the Lola Type 70 Mk. III sports-racing car. This revolutionary feature means that entrants in both European G.T. events and American Can Am sports car races can substantially reduce running expenditure by converting the sports car into its G.T. version, and vice versa.

"The sleek low drag G.T. body, designed in conjunction with Specialised Mouldings Ltd is the result of extensive wind tunnel testing".

Thus enthused Lola's sales literature and two examples of the new coupe were to be inspected at the January '67 Racing Car Show, Surtees' Aston Martin car accompanied by a sister Chevrolet machine, the latter sitting nearby on Lola Cars Ltd's own stand. They caused a stir, looking quite unlike rival Sports-Prototypes.

Lola had not previously employed wind tunnel testing so its latest coupe shape represented a new departure, something of a journey into the unknown. Tony Southgate recalls that he travelled down to London at Broadley's behest to try tufting a 25% model in the City University wind tunnel. He did this with the help of Polish Professor Scibor-Rylski who later wrote the book 'Road Vehicle Aerodynamics' (Pentech, 1975) which became a standard reference on production car design.

The T70 coupe body had started as a sketch by Broadley - straight from his head - and it was refined with the assistance of Specialised Mouldings' boss Peter Jackson and his aerodynamicist Jim Clark, aside from the inputs of Scibor-Rylski, Southgate and fellow Lola draughtsman Mike Smith. Ultimately the coupe's form was the shape

The coupe body version of the T arrived at the Janua '67 Racing Car Sh (previous spre where both As Martin and Ch rolet versions were display. Pictured the Small Bl customer car on Lola Cars Ltd. sta

that looked right to Broadley and that was a shape which cut right across conventional wisdom.

It was generally accepted that a coupe tail should slope down from the cabin roof to a spoiler at wheel arch height. This approach plus a streamlined quarter sphere windscreen led to the characteristic whale-shaped superstructure of the Fords and Ferraris that fought Le Mans in '66.

Basic aerodynamic theory tells us that the whale shape - a bisected teardrop - is the best option for minimum drag. A teardrop has the lowest drag co-efficient of all possible three dimensional forms in free air. Its long tapering tail encourages the boundary layer air to stay attached rather than separate causing drag-inducing turbulence, guiding it back towards its original state thus leaving the smallest possible turbulent wake. The turbulent wake is the invisible parachute that retards the progress of each and every car.

Although the T70 had a fashionable narrow superstructure, behind its cabin its tail did not slope away on the teardrop principle. It was almost horizontal, ending only just below cabin roof height. Running a horizontal tail was - for sheer practicality - a spyder practice. In terms of basic aerodynamics, a horizontal tail implied higher drag with greater stability since it generated a significant measure of downforce.

As we have seen, the Ford Mk.II had been measured as having a co-efficient of drag of Cd Ç 0.35 with less than 150lb. downforce at the rear wheels at 200m.p.h. Comparable figures for the new Lola coupe were a drag co-efficient of Cd Ç 0.47 with rear downforce in the region of 500lb. at 200m.p.h. Both sets of figures were measured from actual cars in the MIRA fixed floor wind tunnel, the Lola figures recorded by Aston Martin.

The T70 coupe's nose shape was directly related to that of the Mk.II Can Am runner though there was no sign of a top-located radiator air exit. That was to be added after the show. There was, however, a central air intake in the nose while other forward facing air intakes were set ahead of the rear wheels, atop the sponson ledges flanking the narrow cockpit canopy and right behind the door. These two intakes were for engine bay cooling.

Starting over the mid located cooling intakes, the rear arches were virtually horizontal, running back to a high rear end flip up rather than a conventional spoiler. Between the two arches a shallow channel ran back through the middle of the superstructure from the firewall bulkhead. The step at the front of this channel allowed Lola to cut a slot into the bulkhead and thus comply with the regulation calling for a rear window of at least 100 x 500mm.

Further, the channel in the high tail left the tops of the inlet trumpets in the open air. The original Lola GT had fed its trumpets from a NACA duct cut in the cabin roof but this had been found to collect air heated by the nose radiator, the warm air staying attached to the windscreen and roof. Down in the shelter of the rear channel, the T70's trumpets could breathe cooler thus denser air.

While the high tail was unconventional, the narrow cockpit canopy state of the art, the T70 was traditional below the waistline with inward curved lower body flanks and an inward curved lower lip to its radiator nose intake. With the radiator tray, the nose offered a full undertray and the floor of the full width tub extended this back to the engine bay which was left open in the interest of cooling. Air was thus encouraged to flow cleanly under the car's belly (which was kept four inches (100mm.) clear of the ground to avoid contact on bumpy circuits). The curved flanks eased the escape of the turbulent vortices created by the shear effect between moving undertray and stationary ground.

The body was a self-coloured g.r.p. moulding by Jackson's company. The windscreen was bonded in with a rubber-based solution making it an integral member of the central coachwork and avoiding the normal protruding rubber grommet. Forming the usual quarter-sphere, it was swept by a large single Lucas wiper. The wiper and its motor were off-the-shelf Lucas parts but there was a mechanical linkage between them rather than the production cable drive.

The doors were gullwing with a positive lock fore and aft via a central handle while their perspex side windows were each provided with a triangular hinged flap for ventilation. Cockpit ventilation is always a major headache with a fully enveloping body and additionally the cockpit was equipped with a fresh air vent as seen on the fascia of Ford production cars, this situated alongside the driver on the righthand torsion box while another inlet introduced cooling air at his feet. Both feeds were taken from the right of the central nose intake while from the left of the intake (on the other side of the radiator) there was an air feed to the base of the screen to keep the screen mist free.

The g.r.p. central body section - running between readily detachable nose and tail panels - comprised three panels aside from the doors, one upper (containing the windscreen) plus one each side below the waistline. Each lower panel wrapped around the flank of its respective torsion box, thus the monocoque was completely concealed. These side panels - largely cosmetic since they hugged the tub - were attached by spire nuts. The upper section was bolted to the pedal box and was bonded to the roll cage which in turn was bolted to the tub. The roll cage comprised a substantial rear hoop of steel, a thinner steel hoop around the screen and two steel tubes to link the two hoops together across the roof.

It was a straightforward job to detach the fully enclosed centre section of the coupe, though conversion to spyder trim was not a rapid process. In contrast, both nose and tail sections were quickly detachable for service access, the former attached by four pip pins, the latter by six. In the nose, a single headlight each side was fitted under a perspex fairing while small holes flanking the central air intake contained auxiliary lights. A vertical tail panel carried the rear lights and had a central ventilation slot through which the exhaust tail pipes emerged. The mandatory spare wheel was set upright in the tail, just ahead of this panel and right behind the gearbox while nominal luggage space was provided over the gearbox.

Optional coupe body aside, the Mk.III T70 was a refined version of the existing Group 7 machine, with its proven all independently sprung monocoque chassis well capable of exploiting the latest developments in low profile, ultra-wide tyres. The Mk.III offered improvements in terms of further weight reduction for the spyder version - through body lightening - the introduc-

tion of driver cooling on the spyder version, better brakes (new were four pot calipers) plus suspension geometry refined in the light of tyre development.

The Mk.III was designed to run on the regular 15 inch diameter rims with front and rear rim widths, respectively, of 8.0 and 10.0 inches, these sizes accepting the latest flat tread offerings from Firestone with respective tread widths of 10.6 and 12.0 inches. In the early Sixties the typical synthetic tread racing tyre had run on a 15 inch rim only 6.0 inches wide with a rear tread width of around 6.0 inches so within the space of a few years tread width had doubled.

Development in 1964 by Dunlop - then the sole Formula One supplier - had seen the advent of the 10 inch wide rear rim, this carrying a tyre with a tread width of 7.2 inches and a section width of 11.8 inches, its sidewalls bulging and its tread domed in traditional style. The section height had meanwhile shrunk to the extent that the aspect ratio had fallen from the traditional 100% to 58%. Significantly, with the low aspect ratio and wider tread the elliptical contact patch became wider than it was long and the effect of this was to call for more precise driving. Much more rubber was on the road and compounds were continually improving.

Firestone arrived in '65 and it wanted still more rubber on the road. In '66 the American company pioneered the flat crown Formula One tyre, which called for chassis designers to re-think suspension geometry. Negative camber was no longer welcome: the flat crown tyre had to be kept square to the ground to develop its full cornering potential. These pioneering tyres were available for all forms of international racing in '67 and were standard issue for the Mk.III.

The Mk.III was based on the familiar full length monocoque with threequarter length torsion boxes flanking the cockpit and cradling the engine and a forward box section extension carrying the front suspension and forming the pedal box. Across the torsion boxes the tub was of U-section with a stressed skin floor between fuel bag carrying boxes, the lids of which formed wide sills either side of the cockpit. There were three major bulkheads - front, firewall and rear - and the engine was bolted in firmly, with the transaxle attached via a Lola magnesium bellhousing and passing through the rear bulkhead.

A low longitudinal stiffening member ran down the centre of the cockpit, dividing driver area from passenger space while there was a stiffening crossbeam between the lower rear pick ups for the front wishbones, this running under the driver's knees. The Mk.III tub also had a new substantial box section running above this, carrying the dash and steering column and further stiffening the tub at the front end of the torsion boxes.

Again the tub was formed of aluminium panels with a steel framework including the inner sides of the torsion boxes. The Aston Martin version required the rear bulkhead to be detachable so as to be able to insert the engine. Since the British engine had a dry sump it required an oil tank and an oil cooler. The tank was situated in the nose, mounted on the front of the pedal box and encroaching on the radiator exit duct while the cooler was set directly behind the water radiator.

An oval-shaped hole in each cockpit sill provided access to the aircraft-style fuel bags. There was one fuel bag in each torsion box with a crossover pipe running behind the seats. A vertical tube projected from the front of each torsion box, running up to emerge through the body just behind the front wheel arch. On the right was a 5.0 inch diameter filler pipe, on the left a 2.25 inch diameter breather. The fuel was lifted from the bags via two Bendix low pressure electric pumps.

The front suspension (and brake arrangement) was carried over from the Mk.II with split upper and lower wishbones. The steel fabricated diamond-shaped main arm of the lower wishbone was picked up by the front bulkhead through a Scheifer self aligning sealed double roller bearing. At the other end it carried the upright via a special ball and cup joint produced by Lola, the cup fixed to the arm. The steel brake reaction leg was picked up at the rear of the pedal box via a rose joint.

The upper wishbone legs were again mild steel and were picked up on the chassis via rose joints while carrying the upright through a proprietary ball and cup joint. The forward leg was chassis-mounted on the same pin as the top of the spring/damper unit. Adjustment at the chassis

on both legs provided camber and caster variation while toe steer through bump and rebound could be varied by altering the height of the rack.

The BMC rack and pinion was mounted on the top of the pedal box behind the front wheel axis. Right behind it was the anti roll bar which was linked to the lower fabricated arm via rose-jointed drop links. The bar was threequarter inch solid steel. The uprights were magnesium with steel hubs running in Timken taper roller bearings, as on the earlier Can Am cars.

No anti dive or anti squat was built into the front or rear suspension, which provided for approximately five inches of wheel movement. The steel springs were not pre-loaded and a representative front spring was 360lb while a representative rear was 380lb.

At the rear the top link provided camber adjustment while the upper radius rod controlled caster and toe in. The steel rear linkages were all rose jointed. The upper link was picked up by the rear bulkhead, as was the reversed lower wishbone while the anti roll bar ran over the top of the bulkhead, this time a 13/16 inch thick steel bar. The upper radius arm was picked up at the firewall bulkhead while the lower radius arm passed through the torsion box then ran in its own tunnel at an angle towards the firewall bulkhead. The tunnel reached the bulkhead, helping stiffen the engine bay but the radius arm pick up was a little way short of it.

At the base of the magnesium upright, a pin running on taper roller bearings held the two legs of the split wishbone and a clevis which picked up the lower radius rod. At the top another pin again held a radius rod clevis and also the single upper link at the front of the upright, with the anti roll bar connection at the back. The upright again carried Timken roller bearings, twin taper bearings separated by a spacer.

The rear hub was two piece, an inner part slotting inside an outer part and passing the drive via splines. The inner part carried the flange that was bolted to a flange on the driveshaft's Hardy Spicer u.j. thereby trapping the brake disc. The outer part carried the wheel drive pegs. Secured by a large three-eared knock-off nut, the front and rear rims were magnesium and were driven by six pins.

The Aston Martin engine had a dry sump in '67, hence the installation of an oil tank and oil coolers behind the water radiator, as seen here on the prototype T70 Mk.III coupe

The brake discs were 12.5" radially ventilated items bolted to a separate bell, with a measure of float permitted. The discs were supplied by Kelsey Hayes and were stopped by forward facing Kelsey-Hayes calipers equipped with Ferodo DS11 pads. The calipers had a cast iron bridge joining the two cylinder housings, this bridge produced by Lola to suit its uprights.

The transaxle was based on an off-the-shelf Hewland gearbox fed from an AP Borg & Beck 71/4" triple plate clutch - or a single plate Scheifer clutch in the case of the Chevrolet car - while roller splined driveshafts were employed. These steel shafts had Hardy Spicer joints at both ends. The gearbox was the four speed LG500, as employed on the Mks.I and II running a clutch-pack differential.

The gear lever was to the right of the driver next to the sill, on which there was a detachable panel carrying the fresh air vent, an ammeter and various switches. The dash was very small, carrying only the tachometer, an oil pressure gauge and a water temperature gauge. The seat was formed in the firewall bulkhead and was covered with lightweight, quickly removable upholstery.

The weight of Surtees' car with the aluminium Aston Martin V8 was in the region of 800 - 820kg, significantly less than that of the Ferrari P3 and the Ford GT40 Mk.II, both of which tipped the scales to over 950kg. The Chevrolet version was no heavier, according to the factory.

Construction of Mk.III coupes at Slough continued through the winter of '67/'68 (left) the car rolling on into the new season virtually unchanged. Note the bare monocoque tub which the coupe shared with the Mk.III spyder. In colour on subsequent pages are various scenes depicting the Aston Martin prototype car at the Nurburgring, finally an atmosphere shot of the '67 Rheims event. Note the fastest lap indicator which shows the name of that very rapid T70 pilot, Paul Hawkins

Improving the Breed

In the right hands the Chevrolet-Lola was a very quick Group 6 motor car. At Francorchamps, at Rheims, at Brands Hatch it showed its paces against the Chevrolet-Chaparral, the Ford-Mirage, Ford Mk.II and the Ferrari P4 and distinguished itself. This season Group 6 lap times reflected three major factors: weight, engine output and aerodynamic performance. The Chevrolet-Lola was not at a disadvantage in any of these areas and clearly enjoyed a strong combination of the three.

At Francorchamps Hawkins carried the Lola challenge in a brand new car: although (in the absence of the Mk.II) fifth on the grid behind the Chaparral, the 5.7 litre Mirage, a works P4 and a customer P3/4, he was as fast as any on race day's wet track. Sadly car owner Epstein did not share his pace.

At Rheims and Brands Hatch the Lola challenge was carried by the likes of Hawkins, Hulme, Surtees, Hobbs and Gardner and the car was the quickest machine at both circuits. At Rheims its superiority over the 7.0 litre factory Ford Mk.II loaned to Ford France was emphatic in spite of the ultra high speed nature of the circuit. Brands Hatch was far more taxing in terms of grip, handling, braking and acceleration yet in the right hands the T70 proved quicker than the 7.0 litre Chevrolet-Chaparral, the 5.7 litre Ford-Mirage and three factory Ferrari P4s.

Power counted for a lot this season, even at Brands Hatch - as witness the Chaparral's third quickest qualifying time there and its straightforward win after the early demise of the two most competitive T70s. The Ford 7.0 litre V8 and the Chevrolet 7.0 litre and 5.9 litre V8s all produced in excess of 500b.h.p, with a very fat power curve to boot. Chaparral ran its special aluminium Big Block 7.0 litre Chevrolet to 7,500r.p.m, higher than any other pushrod en-

gine for an advantage over the Chevrolet-Lola and the Ford Mk.II of perhaps 50b.h.p. On the other hand, the 5.7 litre Ford employed by the Mirage team produced little more than 450b.h.p. and its 100b.h.p. deficit compared to the Chaparral perhaps helps explain its lack of form at Brands Hatch. More importantly, though, the Mirage carried a considerable weight penalty over all its Brands Hatch rivals. The 5.7 litre engine was a major advance over the 5.0 litre Ford in terms of a significantly wider power band but was only worth 20b.h.p. or so at peak power speed.

The 5.0 litre Ford and the 5.9 litre Small Block Chevrolet were the most efficient pushrod engines, producing over 12.5b.h.p. per litre per 1000r.p.m. where the other American power plants managed no more than 11.5b.h.p. per litre per 1000r.p.m. on 100/102 octane fuel. The Small Block Chevrolet was also effective thanks to a wide power band. Its representative 500b.h.p. at 6,750r.p.m. was comparable horsepower to that seen by the 7.0 litre Ford at 6,400r.p.m. whereas the 5.7 litre Ford ran to 7,000r.p.m. for around 460b.h.p. However, employing cross-over exhaust systems for maximum exhaust tuning potential, both Fords had ample mid range power. All the American engines offered a generously fat power curve but the Ford V8s had to pull well over 1000kg. (even the lighter Mk.IV tipped the scales to 1150kg.) whereas the Chevrolet-Lola came in at just under 1000kg.

The Chaparral was lighter still - below 900kg. - thanks partly to its lightweight aluminium 7.0 litre Chevrolet which came direct from the GM Tech Centre with around 575b.h.p. to its credit. There was the key difference between the Chevrolet-Lola efforts and the Chaparral team: Chaparral had the right connections.

In '66 Chaparral had used Small Block Chev-

DIARY

Le Mans (F) April 10
Le Mans Test Weekend

The ACO made its public road-based circuit open for eight and threequarter hours on Saturday and for another five and a half hours on Sunday. Ford and Ferrari were present in strength, the latest three valves per cylinder P4 version of the 4.0 litre Maranello V12 Prototype setting the early pace, well under the '66 lap record of 210.6 seconds. Ferrari had two examples on hand, one open, one closed while Ford had a Mk.II plus its new narrow-superstructure, low frontal area Mk.IV design. On Saturday the Mk.IV was carefully dialled into the special requirements of Le Mans and proved fastest on the Mulsanne if not quickest around the lap.

Ford played with tail fins for the new 7.0 litre car, to no obvious effect. Driven by Bruce McLaren, it was clocked at 205m.p.h, a comparable speed to that of the Mk.II while the best P4 recorded 198m.p.h. A P4 in the hands of Lorenzo Bandini wound up with the quickest Saturday time at 205.5 seconds. However, Motor Sport's correspondent Denis Jenkinson remarked: "McLaren was confident of beating the Ferrari lap speed any time he wanted to, knowing how much he still had in reserve and estimated that he could pull 215m.p.h. along the straight".

That was not put to the test since Sunday was wet and Ford let its drivers register only a few cautious laps, mindful of Walt Hangsen's fatal accident testing a Mk.II in the wet the previous year. Meanwhile, John Surtees continued to pound along in the Aston Martin-Lola he was sharing with David Hobbs. In Jenkinson's words: "Surtees was doing some impressively fast motoring in the rain, proving that there was not much wrong with the Lola part of the all British combine".

The Lola was running a new five speed LG500 and at first there had been a balky third gear selection to sort, then the team had played with nose tabs and higher rear spoilers. Although the car was reluctant to pull over 6,000r.p.m. whereas it was intended to run to 6,500r.p.m this weekend, Surtees had then put in a splendid 211.9 seconds Saturday afternoon lap and with Sunday's wet conditions that stood as third fastest time of the weekend, behind Bandini and Mike Parkes' clockings in a shared P4. In the wet, Surtees lapped over six second faster than the opposition, underlining the T70 Coupe's good grip and handling.

The Lola's Saturday time was even more meritorious in view of the lack of revs which had restricted Mulsanne speed to around 186m.p.h. Suspecting the chassis aerodynamics might be making it difficult for the carburettor-equipped Aston V8 to breathe by creating a low pressure area over the trumpets, the channel in the rear deck had been blanked off, above and around the trumpets, to no real effect. Different trumpets had also been tried to no avail. Towards the end of the weekend Surtees had the passenger side door blow off at Terte Rouge, then the engine started playing up, one carburettor "blowing", perhaps due to a valve problem. Nevertheless, it had been an encouraging outing - aside from the lack of revs, and the fact that the all too new engine had also been running hot...

Spa Francorchamps (B) May 1
Francorchamps 1000Kms.
Hawkins/Epstein .... Q:5 /R:4
de Udy/de Klerk .... Withdrew

Since the Test Weekend a further round of the World Championship had been held, the Monza 1000kms. In this event Ferrari had scored a one-two success in the absence of Ford, the rapid aluminium 7.0 litre V8 engined Chevrolet-Chaparral 2F breaking its driveshaft and two new J.W. Automotive (JWA) Mirages also retiring. The Mirage was a lightened (still over 1000kg.) and more aerodynamic Group 6 version of the GT40 equipped with a 5.0 litre displacement Fairlane engine.

Ferrari sent just one P4 to Belgium while supporting two P3/4 customer cars which had '66 style 4.0 litre V12 engines and '67 bodywork, together with the latest suspension tweeks. The winged Chaparral was out again and JWA had a 5.7 litre V8 engined Mirage for home hero Jacky Ickx backed by a regular 5.0 litre machine.

The two Small Block-T70s present should have been joined by the prototype Aston Martin car but Lola Racing withdrew. The private machines were those owned by Jackie Epstein and Mike de Udy and were identical save for de Udy having the new LG500 five speeder and a 5.5 litre engine whereas Epstein had a 5.9 litre engine.

Sadly de Udy shunted at La Source on the first lap of practice, sidelining his brand new car with damaged steering and front suspension. Meanwhile, Paul Hawkins went very well in the Epstein car, the brand new coupe proving very stable. The c.w.p. failed, but towards the end of practice by which time Hawkins had put the car fifth on the grid behind the Chaparral (pole), the Ickx Mirage, the P4 and the quickest P3/4, this qualified by another Belgian driver.

The two local heros, Ickx and Willy Mairesse, led the opening laps through a rain storm, chased by Parkes in the works P4, Mike Spence in the 2F and Hawkins. Having no experience of running a winged car in the wet, constructor Jim Hall had advised Spence to soft pedal and on the fifth lap Hawkins went ahead of him to harry Parkes, "the Lola obviously handling extremely well in the wet,

Diary continues on page 52

rolets based on a prototype linerless aluminium block, that item offering a weight saving in the region of 50kg. with excellent heat rejection. The new aluminium 7.0 litre V8 with staggered valves was light, potent and reliable, even on the 100/102 octane fuel mandatory for endurance racing. For its part, Ferrari pitched in with around 450b.h.p. at 8,000r.p.m. With twin overhead camshafts and three valves per cylinder its 4.0 litre V12 was the most sophisticated '67 engine and that is reflected in its output of 14b.h.p. per litre per 1000r.p.m. Ferrari likewise enjoyed a healthy power curve, with good fuelling over a wide range of engine speed ensured through its advanced exploitation of fuel injection.

However, this high technology proved insuf-ficient to counter rivals armed with 7.0 litre sledgehammers. With a significant power defi-cit compared to the pushrod giants and no aero-dynamic advantage Maranello had to look to its modest weight of 965kg. - a considerable edge over the Fords. Nevertheless, at Le Mans Ford proved simply too strong for Ferrari - primarily due to a top speed advantage in the region of 15m.p.h. - while at Brands Hatch the Italian car

was overshadowed by the lighter American engined machinery. The Chaparral and Lola were of comparable weight and had greater power and more advanced aerodynamics.

Both Chaparral and Lola had more advanced aerodynamics than either the Ford or the Ferrari challengers. The Ford and Ferrari designs were conventional enough with the Mk.IV Ford scor-ing over its Mk.II stablemate in terms of lower drag, thanks primarily to a narrower super-structure. The prototype of the Mk.IV - the so called 'J Car' of 1966 - had a high tail but the '67 derivative had a conventional rear end sloping down to a tail spoiler at rear wheel arch height. Significantly, though, the Mk.IV had a low nose and slab sides to help dissuade air from flowing to the underbody region. Ford had found air 'wedging' under the car to be a major contribu-tion to total lift.

Wind tunnel tests by Ford had found the Mk.II producing 153kg. (337lb.) drag at 120m.p.h. for a front axle lift of 65kg. and a rear axle nega-tive lift of 36kg. In contrast, at 120m.p.h. the Mk.IV produced a drag of only 112kg. for a front axle lift of 25kg. and a rear axle lift of 18kg, these confirmation of what Surtees had demonstrated at Le Mans", as Jenkinson put it.

Hawkins got by the P4 eventually and went after Mairesse, who in turn was closing on Ickx. Alas, before the anticipated three way battle could be joined the Lola dived into the pits for fuel. Epstein did not have Hawkins' pace and the car fell back during its second stint, to the extent that it was in seventh place at half distance. However, the 2F had fared worse, its engine having been reluctant to restart. When Hawkins got back in the Lola he started making up ground again and renewed rain after a drying spell helped his cause. Alas, there was an unscheduled stop to take on oil, but car kept on running strongly.

Impressively, Hawkins got back on terms with the fourth placed works Ferrari, only to require another stop for oil. At its final stop Lodovico Scarfiotti took over the P4 some way ahead of Hawkins but the delayed flying green Lola came back and caught the red car on the very last lap, albeit two laps down on the winning Ickx/Dick Thompson Mirage following the delays. In the words of Autosport's Patrick McNally: "Hawkins, driving better than I have ever seen him do... took fourth place overall by passing the Italian in an enormous slide at the kink before Stavelot".

Cefalu (I) May 14
Targa Florio
Epstein/Dibley .... R:NR

On paper, the classic Sicilian road race was a battle between a lone works Ferrari P4, a private P3/4, Chaparral's 2F and the fastest two litre cars since the Epstein Lola - the only other big banger - was being raced by two amateurs for the sheer fun of it. Hawkins had accepted a drive in a factory Porsche. The most competitive of the small fry were a factory Ferrari Dino V6, four works Alfa Romeos and six of the works Porsches, which included three 2.2 litre machines in view of the chance for outright success on the mountain course.

In testing (on open roads) the Lola suffered a split fuel bag but this was replaced in time for practice. Practice did not affect the starting order, though it confirmed the Lola was no threat. Worse, Epstein brought the car in the end of the first lap of the race complaining of engine overheating and gear change difficulties.

On the second lap local hero Nino Vaccarella made a rare error and crashed the P4 while the rapid factory Dino also shunted. That left Porsche's finest fighting the P3/4 as the Chaparral team adopted a careful pace. Meanwhile, BOAC pilot Hugh Dibley had done the second lap in the T70 only to find serious oil surge problems and even more serious gearbox woes. Lacking third and fourth gear, the car had to be pushed away.

The Chaparral also succumbed to transmission woes, as did the P3/4, leaving Porsche the winner with its nimble 2.2 litre Prototype, Hawkins sharing the winning car with Rolf Stommelen.

Nurburgring (D) May 28
Nurburgring 1000Kms.
Surtees/Hobbs .... Q:2 /R:NR

Just over one week before Le Mans scrutineering, Lola Racing entered the prototype Aston Martin car for Surtees and Hobbs to share in Germany's gruelling World Championship event. The injection engine was now installed and the car had reverted to the original tail spoiler area, though small front tabs were matched by similar ones behind the rear wheel arches. Ford and Ferrari were absent but both Mirage and Porsche were out again, together with the Chaparral 2F. Phil Hill/ Spence drove the 2F, Ickx/Richard Attwood the lead 5.7 litre Ford V8 engined Mirage which was backed by a 5.0 litre car. Porsche again was running six of its nimble little cars, hoping to profit should the four big bangers wilt.

In qualifying, Spence was fastest with the first 100m.p.h. lap of the 'Ring while JWA lost its second string 5.0 litre Mirage in a shunt. The Aston Martin-Lola distinguished itself with a lap less than 1.5m.p.h. slower than that of the 2F. This, in the words of Jenkinson: "Surtees did without sticking his neck out, and as this was the first race... it was most encouraging". The only drama had been a loose wheel that tucked itself up under the arch: Hobbs had then been extremely lucky to keep the car on the track.

First and second in the Le Mans-style line up, both the Chaparral and the Lola made slow starts, as did the Mirage. The drivers dashed across the track, only for Surtees to have his engine stall, the Mirage prove reluctant to fire while the Chaparral also remained motionless as Hill did up his seat belts on the strict instructions of Hall. The Porsches led at the end of the first 14 mile lap. Surtees was down in twelfth place but he was soon up to seventh, ahead of the Mirage. Meanwhile, Hill had taken the Chaparral through to second, which he thought was first place having miscounted the number of Porsches!

Further back, Surtees settled down to a careful pace, content to watch developments ahead, secure in the knowledge that his car likewise was comfortably quicker than the Porsches. Alas, on lap seven, as he engaged fifth gear attacking the daunting Fuchsrohe downhill swerves the right rear wishbone broke. In a series of lock to lock slides he somehow brought the car to rest without hitting anything.

Subsequently the Chaparral and the Mirage also retired (again transmission

Diary continues on page 54

lift figures insignificant given a car weight in excess of 1000kg. At 220m.p.h. - the target Mulsanne speed - drag was 378kg. with front and rear axle lifts of 86kg. and 60kg. respectively. In the event, the Mk.IV ran the Mulsanne at a 213.1m.p.h. best compared to a best of 206.2m.p.h. for the Mk.II with an identical engine. In spite of its lack of downforce, following some aerodynamic trimming, McLaren reported that Ford had achieved "hands off" stability for the Mk.IV on the Mulsanne, even in a crosswind.

At Rheims, the Mk.II could not keep up with the Chevrolet-Lola and it is doubtful if the Mk.IV would have lapped this French circuit any quicker than the 5.9 litre T70 Coupe. At Rheims there was a 180m.p.h. sweep after the pits and here the British car scored over its American rival thanks to superior high speed, aerodynamically-assisted grip. The downforce generated by the Lola T70 Coupe's high tail was very significant in sweeping curves.

The ultimate in downforce in '67 was enjoyed by the Chaparral 2F with its distinctive aerofoil. For maximum tyre-loading effect the Chaparral wing (a simple aerofoil section, without lateral fences) was again mounted directly to the rear uprights and it was set high above the body in undisturbed air. Also following the 2E, to minimise drag on the straight the driver was able to control the wing's angle of attack. Since the aerofoil was mounted on the wheel side of the springs, the body did not feel the downforce it generated.

Like Ford, Chaparral discouraged air from flowing under its body, having a low set nose

for the Chevrolet car) and Porsche won another World Championship race in spite of its lack of litres (Hawkins this time sharing the second placed car).

Le Mans (F) June 11
24 Heures du Mans
Surtees/Hobbs Q:13/R:NR
Irwin/de Klerk Q:25/R:NR

Although there had been talk of three Aston Martin cars, only two were prepared for the T70's Le Mans debut, the familiar prototype joined by a brand new example, both running five speed gearboxes and factory-tended fuel injection engines. A modified tail was aimed at higher Mulsanne speed. The new car was driven by Surtees and Hobbs while Chris Irwin shared the second car with Peter de Klerk, Pedro Rodriguez no longer part of the Lola Racing effort and driving a NART customer Ferrari P3/4. De Klerk was a South African who had been a mechanic for the team at the test weekend.

Le Mans scrutineering found the two Aston Martin-Lolas opposed by nine serious Ford entries and seven serious Ferrari entries, plus a pair of Chevrolet-Chaparrals. The Ford armada consisted of four Mk.IVs and three Mk.IIs running the 7.0 litre engine plus the two Mirages, both of these now with the 5.7 litre V8. Ferrari had three factory P4s (one a spyder) backed by a customer-run P4 and three customer run P3/4s. Both Chaparrals were examples of the familiar 7.0 litre 2F model with its distinctive wing.

Phil Hill's Chaparral set the early qualifying pace, running 207.4 seconds on Wednesday then going 204.7 seconds on Thursday as Ford grappled with a problem of cracked windscreens on the Mk.IVs. That looked like the pole time until after dark when McLaren - with a sheet of plastic behind a cracked screen - took a Mk.IV for the first and only time in qualifying down the Mulsanne at over 210m.p.h. He clocked 204.4 seconds for the honour of Ford. The best Ferrari was Parkes' P4 on 208.9, only seventh, Maranello overshadowed by the 7.0 litre runners.

Hampered by Aston Martin head gasket problems, Surtees ran 213.7 seconds for 13th quickest, the twelve cars ahead either 7.0 litre American V8 or 4.0 litre Ferrari V12. Surtees was 2.5 seconds clear of the Mirage challenge, which was also engine-troubled and consequently reverted to 5.0 litre race engines. Nevertheless, Surtees was almost two seconds from his Test Weekend best, though Ferrari was also slower while the Ford pole was not as quick as had been anticipated. Ford airfreighted in modified screens for the race.

Rodriguez was quickest off the mark but Hawkins soon put his Mk.II into the lead while Surtees finished the first lap an encouraging sixth behind three Fords and two Ferraris, the Chaparrals having been slow in getting underway. On the second lap Surtees came through seventh, having been passed by McLaren, who had also made a slow start. Alas, at the end of the third lap Surtees trundled into the pits with a holed piston.

A couple of laps later, in came Irwin with the injection pump malfunctioning. With its drive repaired he restarted, only to make frequent repeat calls as the engine ran hot and rough, before retiring with a seized main bearing as a consequence of a broken crankshaft damper. The race was less than one hour old and the Aston Martin challenge was over.

As expected, this race was a battle between the 7.0 litre Fords, the Chaparrals and the Ferraris; Mirage found trouble after an hour or so. Running around 212m.p.h. on the Mulsanne, the Mk.IV Ford proved too fast for the Ferraris - which could not exceed 200m.p.h. - and (with strength in numbers) on average more reliable than the Chaparrals. The Dan Gurney/A.J. Foyt Mk.IV emerged victorious. Ferrari took worthy second and third places (Parkes/Scarfiotti and Mairesse/Jean Blaton) with the McLaren/Mark Donohue Mk.IV fourth, 250 miles down after delays. No other big banger was left in serious contention after 24 hours run at a punishingly fast pace.

Rheims (F) June 25
12 Heures de Reims
Surtees/Hobbs .... Q:2 /R:NR
Hawkins/Epstein .... Q:1 /R:NR
de Udy/Dibley .... Q:6 /R:NR
Hulme/Gardner .... Q:3 /R:NR

The Aston Martin agreement went only so far as Le Mans. Following the Le Mans debacle, Surtees lost no time in replacing the British V8 in his newer chassis with a 5.9 litre Small Block Chevrolet, this again driving through an LG500-based five speed transaxle.

Three privately owned Small Block-T70s were attracted to the prestigious Rheims non-championship Group 6 endurance race, which featured the entry of a Ford Mk.II, the Hawkins/Bob Bondurant Le Mans car. The early Le Mans leader, this Ford had been back to the States for an overhaul and, lent to Ford France, it was now in the hands of Jo Schlesser and Guy Ligier. Ferrari was represented by David Piper's ageing P2/3, which was co-driven by Jo Siffert. The rest of the field comprised Group 4 cars - GT40s and 250LMs - and smaller capacity machinery, somewhat overshadowed on the Rheims high speed blind.

Thus, Lola was looking strong. The Lola Racing entry was backed by the private machines of Epstein (now with a five speeder), de Udy and Sid Taylor. The Taylor car carried a 5.5 litre Chevrolet feeding through a five speed LG500. In it, Grand Prix star Denny Hulme was

Diary continues on page 56

For sheer speed at Rheims in '67 there was nothing to match the Chevrolet-Lola T70. This is the Hulme/Gardner car which had a four lap lead when it broke a water pump pulley just before half distance.

intake and slab sided sponsons. In fact, the rear of the high tailed but spoilerless body generated a small amount of lift while the front created downforce. Consequently, as speed increased the entire body pitched forward and this had the effect of reinforcing the creation of downforce at the front axle. At 150m.p.h. the downforce was sufficient to fully compress the front springs.

One way to avoid locking the front suspension solid would have been to have fitted a spoiler to the rear of the body but this implied a drag penalty. Jim Hall had a more elegant solution which left the rear deck airflow unchecked: a trap door in the floor of the nose. This was spring loaded and was designed to open at 140m.p.h. to bleed air into the underbody region, thus creating nose lift. It was effective, and induced progressive understeer.

For all its aerodynamic trickery, low weight and high power the Chaparral 2F did not overshadow the Lola T70 or its other rivals, though it collected a good number of lap records over the season. It was a car in advance of its time and it clearly had the greatest development potential of all the '67 Big Bangers. However, in '67 Chap-

arral had a very ambitious programme - contesting all World Championship events, unlike Ford, Ford-Mirage or Ferrari - and it was only just starting to scratch the surface of the potential of its new technology. The fact that its front suspension could not take the downforce generated by the body showed that its chassis technology was not yet as advanced as its aerodynamics.

Given tyre developments at this time, cornering forces were reaching 1.3 g without the assistance of aerodynamic aids. With the Chaparral aerofoil the potential was far higher than that but even 1.3 g was venturing far into the unknown. The Chaparral was a bold step into an even further distant uncharted region and the team had to proceed with caution. A straightforward example: at Francorchamps it won pole but in the race day rain it had to watch others disappear as it cautiously trod a treacherously wet surface for the first time ever using a wing.

The Chaparral 2F was a car before its time: the Lola T70 was State of the Art, aside from its traditional underbody treatment. The aforementioned high speed grip was the proof of the excellence of its aerodynamics. The key was its

55

backed by Frank Gardner, a talented Australian all-rounder. Thus, with Hawkins back in the Epstein car the Lola challenge was headed by five professional drivers.

Practice started on Wednesday and was over three days, few teams venturing out the first day. Surtees and Hulme did circulate, Hulme quickest on 131.3 seconds. On Thursday he improved this to 129.1 seconds while Hawkins was next on 129.4 seconds, Surtees trailing on 130.8 seconds while the Mk.II did 132.2 seconds. Unhappy with his engine, overnight Surtees had a replacement 5.5 litre unit fitted.

The Taylor car did not appear on Friday and after fitting small nose tabs Surtees went to the head of the queue with an impressive 128.4 second clocking. However, in the closing stages Hawkins put in a flyer: 127.9 seconds. Thus, the Epstein car headed the line up for the midnight Saturday start, Hawkins ahead of Surtees and Hulme. The Ford Mk.II had got down to 130.1 seconds for fourth place, the last of the quick runners. The de Udy Lola lapped in 138.7 seconds, the P3/4 in 139.6 seconds, these cars overshadowed by the second Piper entry, a 250LM driven by Richard Attwood and Lucien Bianchi that set the Group 4 marker at 138.1 seconds.

Bianchi made a super start but couldn't hold the fast boys back for long, the leaders at the end of the first lap Hawkins, Surtees, Schlesser and Hulme with the 250LM next up. The first two Lolas started drawing away, then Schlesser pitted with a door fastening problem. With Dibley displacing the 250LM, that left Lola filling the first four positions, chased by the two Piper cars.

While Hawkins eased away from Surtees - putting in a record 130.5 second lap in spite of the darkness and a full tank of fuel - Dibley hit electrical trouble, losing a lot of laps. Meanwhile, Schlesser found further trouble in the form of a sticking throttle. At the one hour mark the leading T70 trio was two laps ahead of the rest of the field, which was led by the Piper 250LM. After two hours the delayed de Udy car had to be retired in view of its continuing electrical malady. Meanwhile, Hulme had fallen a lap down on Hawkins.

Two minutes away from the quarter distance mark, Surtees shot into the pits for attention to his engine. To no avail: the crankshaft had broken. One minute from the quarter distance mark, Hawkins swept in to hand over to Epstein. Epstein couldn't get any gears, the bellhousing had cracked. Hawkins told Autosport: "I was only stroking it, too, that car's capable of 127 seconds even in the dark".

With a third of the race run the surviving Hulme/ Gardner T70 was four laps up on the steady Piper 250LM. However, at 5.35am. the Lola broke its water pump drive belt crankshaft pulley. Parts had to be borrowed from the de Udy car, the repair costing half an hour and dropping it to sixth, well out of contention. Meanwhile, the troubled Mk.II Ford had overtaken the Piper 250LM. At 7.30 the 250LM retired and the Lola ominously took on water. Half an hour later it required more and at 8.20 it was retired, its V8 well cooked. The Mk.II went on to win while Piper's P2/3 finished second.

Brands Hatch (GB) July 30

BOAC 500 Six Hour race
Surtees/Hobbs .... Q: 2/R:NR
Brabham/Hulme .... Q: 1/R:NR
de Udy/Westbury Q:14/R:NR

The final round of the World Championship for Manufacturers found both Ferrari and Porsche in with a chance of the crown and consequently both marques were strongly represented. Realistically, the fight for victory had to be between Ferrari, Ford-Mirage, Chevrolet-Chaparral and Chevrolet-Lola, though Brands Hatch's twists gave Porsche a fighting chance. Ferrari sent three P4s, all in spyder trim and backed by a P3/4 while the Mirage and Chaparral teams sent one car apiece. Mirage was running a 5.7 litre engine once more while Porsche was running three of its five cars in 2.2 litre trim.

The three Lolas were familiar cars, those of Lola Racing (again with a 5.5 litre engine), Taylor (running Goodyear tyres, this helping put Jack Brabham alongside Hulme) and de Udy, who was joined in the cockpit by hillclimb star Peter Westbury. The Epstein car was meanwhile en route to Australia for a 12 hour race.

The early qualifying pace was set by Hulme, chased by Spence in the 2F, the two fastest P4s and Surtees, who was not happy with his suspension following some modifications. The next day started wet but dried right at the end when Surtees equalled Hulme's provisional-pole time of 96.6 seconds. The 2F was next up on 97.4 seconds, driveshaft failure costing its planned pole bid while the two quickest Ferraris wound up sharing 97.8 seconds. The Mirage was out of the picture but the two quickest Porsches weren't far behind on 98.2 seconds!

Surtees made the best start with Hawkins' P4 slotting into second ahead of Scarfiotti's similar car, Graham Hill's cheeky Porsche, Spence in the 2F then the slow-starting Hulme Lola. On the second lap Surtees started falling back: his carburettors were flooding and he was soon in the pits for attention to them. Meanwhile, Spence came through to second, followed by Hulme. On the sixth lap Hulme leapfrogged into the lead, and within a lap he had pulled the length of the pits straight over Hawkins, who was soon further demoted by Spence.

Meanwhile, Hulme had cut a record

Diary continues on page 58

high rear deck. Its unique body shape endowed it with sufficient downforce front and rear for good grip and handling and excellent all round driveability. Good aerodynamics plus a Can Am proven chassis allowed the T70 Coupe to use its tyres well. That much was evident in the wet at Francorchamps: Hawkins was closing on that master of the circuit, and master of the wet Jacky Ickx when he handed to Epstein.

Hawkins later told Autosport: "I didn't have much time in practice to get the car set up properly, but it certainly went well in the race. What a wonderful car to drive! It went exactly where you wanted it to, and you could slide it confidently at 140-150m.p.h. in the wet. It didn't seem to be affected by side winds or other things that affect most cars, like uneven road surfaces or bumps in the middle of corners".

Francorchamps was a very fast venue, Rheims even faster - the T70s were touching 200m.p.h. on the Paris/Soissons Route Nationale - yet there were none of the dramas that accompanied the GT40 in its early days. Small front tabs and rear spoilers as fitted by Surtees and some customers were a normal trimming-out of the aerodynamic balance. The T70 body shape was basically right from the outset and in spite of power in the region of 500b.h.p. and weight of less than 1000kg. the machine was easy to handle, stable, vice-free and forgiving. In that respect it was an ideal machine for the privateer.

It was also a sign that the T70 did not suffer from having a productionised chassis. With its steel and aluminium tub it had a torsional rigidity of 3200lb.ft. per degree compared to 10,000lb.ft. per degree for the hefty steel tub of the grossly overweight Mk.II. The figure for the T70 was comparable to that for the g.r.p. based tub of the 2F and was possibly superior to that for the Ferrari P4, which had a plated spaceframe and employed alloy rather than g.r.p. body panels. This was essentially the same chassis carried by the earlier P2 and P3 models: it was inexpensive, very practical and year after year did the job. In '66 and '67 Brabham won the Formula One World Championship using a spaceframe chassis. Further, Ferrari did not have the budget of Ford.

Ford saved some weight in the Mk.IV by switching to a complex and highly expensive aluminium honeycomb tub at no loss of torsional rigidity. However, the composite material proved very difficult to work and would have been impractical, and also too expensive, for a customer car such as the T70. Further, the Mk.IV was still too heavy with at least 15% more weight than any of its rivals. Any performance advantage in the way of superior wheel control Ford could have hoped to have gained through torsional stiffness it lost through excessive weight. And weight affects braking and acceleration as well as cornering, and does nothing to assist the quest for reliability.

Reliability was the major challenge of all the Big Bangers of '67. The major weakness of the Chevrolet-Chaparral was its transmission. The 2F ran a three speed version of the clutchless transmission developed by GM that had been more dependable in previous years. Faced with 7.0 litre torque and endurance racing it became the Chaparral's Achilles Heel. Essentially it was a conventional gearbox with straight cut gears selected by dog clutches, Hewland style, but fed through a fluid coupling rather than a conventional clutch. This coupling was able to slip when engine speed fell below 5,000r.p.m. so that there was no need for a clutch pedal. To change gear the driver merely feathered the throttle.

The GM transmission was not a great advantage: a sensitive driver could operate a Hewland without the clutch. With its 7.0 litre engine Chaparral considered three speeds adequate whereas Ford ran four speeds, Ferrari five. The Ferrari gearbox was a purpose built in house production whereas the Ford unit was a production based model. Nevertheless, the Ford gearbox was well proven and dependable whereas the GM gearbox was not. The Chevrolet-Lola also found it hard to keep its transmission running.

In particular, the Small Block-T70 Coupes suffered a number of disconcerting c.w.p. breakages (including Epstein at Francorchamps, de Udy at Brands Hatch and Lola Racing at Croft). Lola and Hewland never got the the bottom of this. A gearbox failure put the Epstein car out of the Targa Florio while at Brands Hatch the Taylor car succumbed to clutch failure after a broken rocker arm had been replaced.

Notable chassis failures were the wishbone

Overleaf, the Epstein/Dibley car is seen on the Targa Florio - not the sort of circuit on which the T70 was in its element. Neither driver was of world class, both racing for the sheer fun of it. Alas, the gearbox failed early on, spoiling their enjoyment.

Diary Continued

97.2 second lap and he settled down with a comfortable margin over the Chaparral. Alas, on lap 23 Hulme slowed dramatically, limping into the pits with a cylinder non-functioning due to a broken rocker arm. This was duly replaced, but 15 minutes were lost. Meanwhile, the Surtees car had lost further ground to its carburettor problem. The third T70 simply wasn't quick enough and at the one hour mark lay two laps down on the 2F, while Surtees was four laps down but now was running cleanly.

Hulme's car wasn't running properly following its valve train repair and was soon to retire due to clutch failure. However, Surtees got well into the groove and at the two hour mark was only two laps down, albeit off the fuel schedule. Then the head gasket started failing and at the three hour mark the gallant effort was five laps back. That became four at the four hour mark, after which a sticking hub caused further delay, then a piston failed due to low fuel pressure. Meanwhile, de Udy had lost more ground when he stopped to attend to a loose door and couldn't restart the engine. A walk to the pits for a new battery was necessary. Eventually, his car succumbed to c.w.p. failure.

The race fell comfortably to the Chaparral, while Ferrari and Porsche battled for second and the Championship. The fastest P4 survived and Ferrari got the position, but by a margin no greater than the time Porsche's chasing 2.2 litre hope (Siffert/McLaren) had lost to an unscheduled brake pad change.

Croft (GB) August 13
Wills Trophy (77.5 miles)
Hobbs .... *Q: 2/R:DQ(1)*
Hulme .... *Q: 1/R:1*
de Udy .... *Q: 6/R:NR*
Wilson .... *Withdrew*

Lola Racing came out with its Brands Hatch car for a final time at Croft Autodrome, a minor British circuit. Although this was only a National Open Groups 4 and 6 event, the organisers had managed to gather a strong Group 6 entry including four T70s, the Piper P2/3 seen at Rheims plus a loaned factory 2.0 litre Porsche (the spare from the BOAC 500) driven by Vic Elford and Brian Redman's rapid BRM-Chevron. Hobbs drove the Lola Racing T70, Hulme the Taylor car, de Udy his own machine while one Max Wilson brought out his own example. The 50 lap Trophy race was preceded by 15 lap heats, one apiece for the Group 6 and the Group 4 runners, the top six plus the next 12 quickest on lap time going forward to the final combined category final.

Hobbs and Hulme were predictably quickest in practice, while Redman was third fastest and the Wilson car broke its c.w.p. which sidelined it. On race morning Hobbs suffered a similar breakage, this costing him a chance of starting the Group 6 heat. Hulme easily won that race after the fast starting Redman had led the first three laps. Hobbs was allowed to join the back of the grid for the final but was ineligible for awards...

The final was wet, Hulme led the early stages but - revelling in the conditions - Elford caught him. Meanwhile, Hobbs was coming through fast and on superior tyres he passed both Hulme and Elford. Hulme then lost almost a lap to Elford switching to the same tyres but came back to take second place to Hobbs, and thus the official victory. Meanwhile, de Udy had retired with a flat battery.

breakage that pitched the Aston Martin car off the 'Ring and the cracked bellhousing that stopped the Epstein car at Rheims. These were one-off failures. To some extent the new car's retirements were "teething troubles" - though the Chevrolet engine was well proven. In total, three of eight retirements from a total of nine Chevrolet starts at Francorchamps, the Targa Florio, Rheims and Brands Hatch were down to the engine.

At Rheims the Lola Racing car suffered a broken crankshaft, at Brands Hatch it suffered piston failure blamed on low fuel pressure. At Rheims the Sid Taylor car overheated after suffering temporary loss of its water pump due to failure of the pump drivebelt pinion on the crankshaft.

Overall, the high rate of Chevrolet-Lola attrition reflects the fact that the cars were run by small teams rather than a major factory. There were four key teams running the Small Block-T70 Coupe: Lola Racing, Sid Taylor (chassis SL73-102), Jackie Epstein (SL73-112) and Mike de Udy (SL73-105), though other examples were distributed around the racing world.

The Lola Racing example was a converted Aston Martin car which appeared at Rheims, after the unhappy Le Mans experience. Taylor also came out at Rheims and a week later gave the model its first major win in the Norisring 200 mile race at Nuremberg in Germany, Frank Gardner at the controls. Gardner later won a national race at Crystal Palace for Taylor. Taylor like Lola Racing ran strong driver pairings (Hulme and Gardner at Rheims, Hulme and Brabham at Brands Hatch) whereas Epstein and de Udy drove their own cars and were not in the same league as the professionals.

Most of the Chevrolet cars followed the early conversion of the Lola Racing prototype Aston Martin car to a five speed LG500. Small nose tabs and a conventional rear spoiler became standard wear as the season wore on while Surtees had his Aston Martin car's special Le Mans tail at Rheims. He also had some suspension tweaks for Brands Hatch, playing with the geometry.

Surtees employed an American Traco-prepared engine, later a British built Alan Smith engine, Smith already fettling the 5.5 litre V8 of the Taylor car. At Brands Hatch de Udy had an

unconvincing 5.3 litre Traco prepared engine
with a relatively short stroke and a 7000r.p.m.
red line. While the standard 5.4 litre Falconer
engine came with Weber 48IDAs, the 5.9 litre
engines run by Surtees and Epstein were equipped
with the bigger Weber 58DC0Es. However, the
supply of them was rapidly drying up.

Not all engines were wet sump: after winning
the poorly supported Australian Grand Prix
Hawkins bought the Epstein car and ran into oil
surge problems at Kyalami, just as Epstein had
done in the Sicilian mountains. Hawkins consequently converted to a dry sump for the remain-
ing three end of season Springbox races. He won
two of those races, those in Cape Town and
Mozambique. Interestingly, in Mozambique de
Udy (winner in July of the poorly supported
Villa Real International in Portugal) tried a cross-
over exhaust system to no obvious advantage.

The various Lola teams generally ran either
Goodyear or Firestone tyres, sometimes Dun-
lops according to preference and sometimes
carried a mixture of makes on the truck. Overall,
the major contenders this season were equally
divided between Goodyear and Firestone tyres,
and even within the Ford camp, one faction was
on Goodyear, the other on Firestone. In the
event, Goodyear won Le Mans with Shelby/
Ford, Firestone the World Championship with
Ferrari.

Meanwhile, the Aston Martin adventure went
unfinished. The brand new V8 offered promising performance given the intention to productionise it, the car clocking some good times in
testing and at the 'Ring. However, the engine
was down on revs and clearly lacking development mileage. In truth, it went to Le Mans with
far too little mileage under its belt. The unhappy
Le Mans race experience gave Aston Martin
cause for some serious development work and
the '68 Group 6 capacity limit of 3.0 litres meant
that the success of this would go untested on the
track, at least for the time being.

The early lack of revs saw the V8 pulling
6,000r.p.m. rather than its intended 6,400r.p.m.
on its maiden run at Snetterton in March, then
at the Le Mans test. That must have given it less
than 400b.h.p. and speed on the Mulsanne was
only 186m.p.h. whereas Ford was running over
200m.p.h. - in the light of which Surtees' lap

*The Aston Mar-
tin-Lola is pictured
here at Le Mans
during the test
(left) and the race.
At the start of the
race Surtees can be
seen joining the
heavy traffic behind
a Ferrari P4 and a
Ford GT40, while
the sister car is
pictured during its
troubled practice.
Note modified
exhaust on the
engine at the test,
compared to the
photograph on page
31 which shows the
original layout.*

times in SL73-101 were encouraging.

The performance of the chassis was unquestionably good in terms of grip and handling as was borne out subsequently by the Chevrolet Coupes, and of course by the Aston Martin car's form at the 'Ring. However, the British engine had shown a narrower than anticipated power band calling for the five speed LG500 gearbox and clearly needed more breath on the Mulsanne, while it was also running hot at the Test Weekend.

The debut run at Snetterton had ended with a badly machined valve spring cracking a tappet and a valve spring broke at the Le Mans test. In the light of these problems Aston Martin started shimming the springs. The lack of full exhaust tuning (with a two plane crank and no pipe crossover) might have accounted for the disappointing width of the power band. At the Test Weekend Lola Racing had different trumpets to play with and tried straightening the exhaust to avoid a nasty kink as it desperately sought higher revs. To no avail.

Makeshift modifications to the tail to try to create high pressure over the trumpets still did not provide the sought after higher r.p.m. on the Mulsanne. However, the 'Ring with the first injection engine was more encouraging, the Aston Martin-Lola looking a very competitive package with its good grip, light weight and reasonable if not over-impressive power level. The injected V8 was only the third race engine built and it was down a little on top end power compared to the Weber version.

Nevertheless, two injected engines were built for Le Mans and straightaway both pulled 6,400r.p.m. on the Mulsanne. Surtees saw 6,700r.p.m. with the aid of a tow and clocked a best of 205.1m.p.h. on the Mulsanne running a revised tail, a large perspex window covering the central channel ahead of a full width adjustable spoiler. This tail - fashioned in alloy and only fitted to Surtees' car - was slightly longer and was more traditional in appearance, Broadley seeking lower drag, sacrificing some downforce. NACA ducts on each side fed the engine.

Since the regulations called for the spare wheel to be replaced during the race, it was stowed horizontally so that it could be pulled out without opening the tail. This allowed the mega-

Surtees at the 'Ring: highly competitive for as long as it lasted. That was so often the case for the T70 Coupe in '67...

phones to be set lower while the luggage space was provided in the back of the wheel arches. At the Test Weekend it had been found that the inertia of the gearbox driven magneto had tended to motor the 'box, making gear shifting more difficult .Consequently, the magneto was now driven off the driveshaft.

Brakes are a major concern at Le Mans since they have time to cool on the long Mulsanne straight before being banged on hard for the tight Mulsanne corner. The thermal shock as the pads attack a cold disc can cause disc cracking. Indeed, in 1965 when radially ventilated discs were used for the first time at the French circuit, both Ford and Ferrari were plagued by cracking, the introduction of ventilation channels causing stress concentration. No simple solution was at hand. In 1967 Ford ducted warm air to its front brakes from the radiator outlet. It was significant, then, that the T70 had big brakes outside of the wheelrim (as usual) and had no brake cooling ducts.

The new Surtees car - SL73/121 - with its alloy tail was not finished until the weekend prior to Le Mans. It was then run at Goodwood on the Monday prior to being shipped on the midnight boat to catch Tuesday's scrutineering. Alas, in practice for the race the injected cars lapped no faster than Surtees had managed at the test.

Surtees was very unhappy with the power level, which he estimated as under 400b.h.p, much less than he had been promised. The NACA ducts fed via curved trumpets and these were suspected of causing a power loss. Worse, in practice the engines in both cars again ran hot. The original car required water every couple of laps and then lost a head gasket in first qualifying while the newer car lost a gasket in the second day's practice.

The team only had one spare engine so the Aston Martin engineers set about rebuilding the two practice units, robbing bits from the spare. It was suspected that the Cooper rings had been shuffling and thus leaking water so the engines were rebuilt with a shim under each ring to supply some pre-load. This was something of a desperate measure and the work was not finished until Friday night. Their engines installed, the cars were tested on the road in the early hours of Saturday.

On Saturday afternoon Surtees' car came in to retire with oil gushing from its tank breather. One exhaust was cold. The plug was removed and it had a piece of aluminium welded to it. The piston was holed. Aston Martin later criticised Surtees' switch for the race from Champion to Marchel plugs, Marchel offering some sponsorship. For his part, Surtees was very unhappy with the engine modifications and later criticised the Aston Martin engineers as talented but prone to squabbling and "muddling".

On the Lola side it is worth noting that Surtees had been very busy with his Honda project, while on the engine front the lead time was clearly too short for a 24 hour race. And overall, the budget was tiny. The late engine modification didn't bear fruit and whether the cause was the head gasket, or the alternative plugs, or the injection timing (allegedly 180 degrees out of phase) or a lack of cooling using the new tail or even the quality of the fuel supplied by the organisers, the upshot was the first retirement of the race.

The older car came in initally with the gear on the camshaft powering the Lucas pump's drive belt having fallen off. This was fixed only for failure of the rubber and metal crankshaft damper to take its toll of the front main bearing. The broken cylinder of the other engine was subsequently repaired and the engine then ran over 24 hours on the test bench. However, it is unlikely that it could have lasted Le Mans in the back of a car. The post race strip down revealed a sorry tale.

On both engines the blocks had twisted, cracking evident around the main bearing supports and the liners and heads out of true. There was clearly a lack of structural rigidity. In the light of this the block was redesigned, stiffer and with better location for the main bearing caps and heads. This finally overcame the head gasket problem. The damper specification was also changed. Racing can improve the breed.

68

Shock from Paris

By the end of '67 Lola had produced over 50 Can Am versions of the T70. However, although with Coupes its total model production had exceeded 50 early in '67 it hadn't been granted the anticipated Group 4 homologation. The CSI had insisted on 50 Coupes and with demand strong Lola had made that its target, tooling up for 50 5.4 litre Small Block examples in the summer of '67. Then came the sudden announcement of the 5.0 litre limit for '68. Announced soon after Le Mans, the Groups 4 and 6 limits of 3.0 litres and 5.0 litres respectively shook the racing world to the very core. Having set up for a homologation run of large capacity Chevrolet Coupes Lola faced severe financial consequences. Cancelled orders confirmed its worst fears.

The announcement came from a meeting held in Paris just days after the Le Mans race, giving manufacturers a lead time half that permitted under International sporting regulations. The lack of notice was justified by the authorities on the grounds of safety, though few accepted that such capacity restrictions would significantly slow the cars. The new ruling had clearly been influenced by the ACO's concern over rising speed at Le Mans, on the Mulsanne and in front of the pits.

Other factors were the pending withdrawal of Ford and the emergence of important French and German 3.0 litre Sports-Prototypes. Matra and Alpine Renault were aspiring to Formula One, thus had 3.0 litre engines under development. Porsche was also known to be working on a 3.0 litre engine, though as a logical progression from 2.0 litres rather than as a Grand Prix project.

Interestingly, Enzo Ferrari publicly complained that the new regulations favoured larger concerns, ones capable of building 50 replicas of a 5.0 litre Group 6 car. Surely no manufacturer would go to that extreme? Behind the scenes Ferrari Technical Director Mauro Forghieri used the sudden regulation change as a means to achieve a single-seater only racing policy: he wanted that for logistical reasons. Influenced by his pressure, Enzo Ferrari pulled out of the '68 World Championship for Manufacturers.

Ford had planned a withdrawal in any case, while Chaparral found itself shut out. Meanwhile, ambitious Porsche Technical Director Ferdinand Piech - nephew of marque founder Ferry Porsche - was talking to Volkswagen, pressing for the means of raising the funding for a 50-off 5.0 litre sports-prototype rather than a one-off 3.0 litre version...

The possibility of a manufacturer producing 50 replicas of a sports-prototype as a means of circumventing the 3.0 litre Group 6 rule had not been considered a serious possibility by the CSI. Faced with a financial crisis Broadley demanded that the T70 Coupe be accepted as a Group 4 car with a 5.0 litre version of the Small Block Chevrolet and this the CSI was prepared to entertain since the old pushrod engine was no more potent than a 3.0 litre Formula One engine. Further, Group 4 cars had a minimum weight limit of 800kg, Group 6 of 650kg.

Thus, in view of Lola's special circumstances, the CSI accepted to homologate the Mk.III Coupe as a 5.0 litre Chevrolet engined, 800kg. Group 4 car as from February 1 1968. This was somewhat ironic since in so doing it was counting Can Am versions, something it had refused to do before. Thus, the model entered Group 4 somewhat belatedly, an obvious Ford GT40 and Ferrari 250LM beater. Those rivals lacked the power of the Small Block while the Ford was too heavy.

World Championship Group 6 racing was another matter altogether given the potential of an almost 20% lighter Formula One engined coupe. By this stage Formula One engine power was creeping over 400b.h.p. - in 5.0 litre guise the Small Block Chevrolet mustered no more than 440b.h.p.

Group 6 projectiles were to be fielded - in the absence of Ferrari - by Alpine Renault, Matra, Porsche - with its new sports car only 3.0 litre engine - and Howmet - pitching in with a turbine propelled 3.0 litre equivalent machine (the equivalency factor simply a CSI 'guestimate'). Meanwhile, Ford of Britain planned a Cosworth-Ford DFV engined car and the JWA team looked to BRM V12 Formula One power for a projected Group 6 contender while running GT40s as a stopgap. Alfa Romeo was also preparing for an eventual move to 3.0 litre Group 6.

At Slough, demand for the Coupe picked up again once homologation was confirmed but there was no works team for World Championship racing. The most serious effort was that of Ecurie Bonnier, the small Swiss-based team run by Swedish Grand Prix privateer Joakim Bonnier. Bonnier bought the Lola Racing prototype car - chassis SL73-101 - and fitted his own 5.0 litre Chevrolet. The distinctive yellow painted private entry was one of half a dozen European based 5.0 litre T70 Coupes pledged to contest at least some of the World Championship races, while actor James Garner's American International Racing effort based two further Group 4 cars in the USA.

Meanwhile, in view of the earlier cancelled Coupe orders Lola had looked to the emerging Formula A single seater class in the USA for 5.0 litre stock block machines, producing a simple spaceframe car with T70 running car, the T140/142. It was still involved in Formula Two and Indy Car racing and Can Am orders were still coming in so the company retained a very good export market across the Atlantic and it opened a third factory unit to cope with demand early in '68.

DIARY

Sebring (USA) March 23
12 Hours of Sebring
Patrick/Jordan .... *Q:4 /R:NR*
de Udy/Dibley .... *Q:9 /R:NR*
Bonnier/Axelsson .... *Q:10 /R:NR*
Guldstrand/Leslie .... *Q:34 /R:NR*

Newly homologated as a Group 4 car, the 5.0 litre Chevrolet-Lola came out in force at Sebring, two entered by James Garner's American International Racing Team, one apiece by Joakim Bonnier and de Udy. Garner's drivers (Merlin 'Scooter' Patrick, Dave Jordan, Dick Guldstrand and Ed Leslie) were all American road racing regulars - Patrick the '66 U.S.R.R.C. 2.0 litre winner - while Bonnier's partner Sten Axelsson was a fellow Swede, little known outside his homeland.

Aside from Chevrolet-Lola, favourites for victory were Porsche and JWA. Porsche was still running its 2.2 litre eight cylinder Typ 907 coupe (the '67 derivative of the Carrera 6) - its three litre engine as yet unready - so badly lacked power. At Daytona for the 24 Hour race at the beginning of February this hadn't stopped its four car team taking a surprise win over JWA, which had enjoyed superior speed but not reliability. The British team had switched its pair of well proven 4.7 litre Ford V8 machines to wider wheels and tyres and this had led to the failure of second gear in the regular ZF transmission on both cars.

Sebring practice showed the 907 to be on the pace at the slower road course, Jo Siffert putting his example on pole, one second faster than the lead Ickx/Redman JWA GT40. Also raising eyebrows was the speed of the unique Howmet TX turbine car which was only two tenths of a second further back. The only other serious runners were Ed Nelson's GT40 which he shared with David Piper, a 3.0 litre Alpine and an old 250LM.

At the start, Siffert was first away and at the end of the first lap three 907s led de Udy and Patrick with the other T70s back amid the assorted modified American production cars that comprised the bulk of the field. On the second lap Patrick got up into third place and he was soon challenging Elford's 907, slotting past on the third lap to set about Siffert. Meanwhile de Udy had come through to fourth. On lap nine Patrick displaced Siffert, having gone under the Porsche pole time in spite of a full fuel load - lapping only 0.4 second from the 7.0 litre 2F's record - while de Udy was now a strong third.

Alas, de Udy required pits attention for a loose exhaust before the one hour mark, at which Patrick led comfortably. Meanwhile, after teething troubles in practice Bonnier's car was still not running properly, pitting regularly to hunt the source of a misfire. Having still led at the two hour mark, in the words of Autosport correspondent Pete Lyons: "the baby-blue Lola shuddered to a halt at the hairpin with its steering disconnected and Patrick scooted back to the pits to collect some tools, losing altogether over an hour and all hope".

The repair was to no avail: the car broke a piston before half distance. Patrick had only the consolation of fastest lap. By half distance the de Udy and the second AIR car had likewise retired, while Bonnier still had a misfire. Eventually it was discovered that the fuel source had been diluted with water and the yellow Lola was parked in disgust. The race fell to Siffert/Herrmann as all the other quick runners met trouble, a second 907 limping home, the others joining Lola, Ford, Howmet, Alpine and Ferrari in the big dead car park.

Brands Hatch (GB) April 7
BOAC 500 Six Hour race
Bonnier/Axelsson .... *Q:7 /R:6*
Charlton/Fisher .... *Q:8 /R:NR*
Epstein/Nelson *Q:33/R:18*

Porsche took a trio of 2.2 litre 907s to Brands Hatch, a circuit to which the car was ideally suited and, indeed, only one rival got in among them in practice, the new Ford F3L. The 3.0 litre Cosworth DFV propelled monocoque coupe designed by GT40 draughtsman Len Bailey and produced by Alan Mann Racing for Ford of Britain was 0.8 second off Siffert's pole in the hands of McLaren. Ickx' fastest Group 4 car was 1.4 seconds further back while Bonnier's quickest T70 was 1.6 seconds further back again, well behind the Howmet.

The Ford was the only new factor in the World Championship contest, the field padded out by amateur Ford and Ferrari Group 4 cars and various 2.0 litre machines. Of the slow Alpine there was no sign, the French team concentrating upon the clashing Le Mans test weekend, at which Lola was represented by Ulf Norinder's new car (which broke its crankshaft before it could get down to business). The Dave Charlton/ Craig Fisher T70 was Sid Taylor's white and green striped machine. The JWA team was down to one car due to the Le Mans clash but team drivers Hawkins and Hobbs drove the former's private GT40 as a second Gulf entry.

The opening laps found Charlton best placed of the T70 fleet, in seventh behind the top six qualifiers and shadowed by Bonnier. On lap seven the Howmet's throttle jammed and the car crashed out, elevating Charlton to sixth, then Bonnier swapped places with him. These two cars continued dicing to the one hour mark, by which time the leading Porsche and Ford F3L had lapped them. The Lola fight was broken up before the first fuel stops, when Charlton got neutral and spun. He spun again after refuelling as gear selection difficulties worsened, this time hitting the bank and putting the car out of action.

Diary continues on page 68

Opportunity Lost

1968 was the year of missed opportunity for the Lola T70 Coupe. There was no consistent World Championship challenge by a Formula One engined Group 6 car. Porsche made the most concerted title bid using its 2.2 litre eight and a late arriving 3.0 litre replacement boxer that could not muster more than 350b.h.p. The field was open for a pushrod engined Group 4 machine to succeed, not withstanding its enforced weight penalty. Sure enough, the old GT40 came through to success after success.

There was one major difference between the GT40 and the Lola T70 World Championship efforts of 1968: J.W. Automotive. No highly professional two car team set out to contest the World Championship for Manufacturers with the 5.0 litre Small Block-T70. Yet it was far lighter and far more aerodynamically advanced than the GT40, and more powerful. In December 1968 Broadley remarked to Autosport that he was looking to set up a works World Championship for Manufacturers team under direct control of the factory; "we are most anxious to get a good car running in Group 4".

But by this stage it was too late to make hay in the sunshine. For 1969 the CSI had vowed to scrap the Group 6 weight limit and to admit pure spyders once again. With Ferrari coming back into the fray, there would be some very quick Group 6 cars in regular contention in '69, unlike this season. Distracted by what Broadley admitted to Autosport had been "commitments in too many directions", Lola had missed its golden opportunity. Chevrolet would have done well to have helped promote a T70-based replacement for its Chaparral bid: instead GM saw Ford win the World Championship, and once again succeed at Le Mans.

The World Championship for Manufacturers might have meant little to the average American

Diary continued

By this stage the Ford prototype had broken and at the two hour mark Axelsson had the yellow Bonnier car sixth, two laps down and behind the three 907s, the Ickx GT40 and Piper's familiar 250LM which was being spiritedly driven by Rodriguez. With the Mexican handing to Roy Pierpoint, the yellow Lola was left fending off the slow starting Hawkins GT40 for fifth place. This became fourth in the fourth hour as the Siffert Porsche was pushed away, victim of wheel bearing failure.

As the afternoon wore on the Hawkins/Hobbs GT40 got the better of the Lola and with only a few minutes of the race to run a flat battery dropped it further back, behind the Piper 250LM and 11 laps down on the race winning GT40 of Ickx/Redman. Meanwhile the dark green Epstein Lola had suffered a split fuel bag and it came home 35 laps down on the winning car, which had only narrowly defeated the two surviving 907s. Indeed, the winning margin was 22 seconds, after a two and a half minute delay for the second placed 907 due to a faulty pad wear warning light.

Nurburgring (D) May 19
Nurburgring 1000Kms.
Norinder/Widdows Q:12/R:NR

The T70 was making a welcome World Championship re-appearance at the 'Ring, not having been represented at the Monza 1000Kms. or the Targa Florio. At Monza the 3.0 litre Porsche 908 had made its debut, giving the German marque enough speed to challenge JWA in spite of the high speed nature of the course. However, development problems, mainly due to engine vibration left the race to the

GT40. Ickx/Redman were delayed by a broken exhaust, then Redman crashed the car leaving Hawkins/Hobbs the victors. The Howmet turbine had gone back home.

In view of its shortcomings, Porsche did not run the new 908 in the Targa Florio, from which JWA abstained. That left a quartet of 2.2 litre 907s challenge a similar number of works Alfa Romeos, one of which had a 2.5 litre V8, the rest 2.0 litre engines. Porsche had won, though not without much drama...

Looking for success on home soil, Porsche brought out two revised 908s for the 'Ring 1000Km. backed by two 2.2 litre 907s, all of these brand new cars. Alfa Romeo this time had a pair of 2.5 litre cars while Alan Mann Racing re-appeared with two of its F3Ls and Alpine Renault brought two cars that it had run without success at Monza. JWA had its familiar GT40s while the T70, JWA's principal Group 4 rival, was that owned by Ulf Norinder and first seen at the Le Mans test weekend. This Swedish-owned car, only two months old, was co-driven by young Englishman Robin Widdows.

Irwin crashed one of the F3Ls heavily in practice, putting himself in hospital with serious head injuries. Meanwhile, Hans Herrmann won pole position in a 907 with Ickx next up. The Lola suffered an unbalanced engine but Widdows drove it with aplomb. His time of 545.7 seconds compared well to a pole time of 512.8 seconds given little lappery. Alas, on race day the engine failed after 50 miles or so, Widdows leaving a black trail of oil over the high Hohe Acht.

The surviving F3L was another early retirement and the race saw an easy win for the Siffert/Elford 908 as Ickx/Hawkins fought the 907s, to finish third overall - the only obstacle to complete Porsche domination. The best Alfa Romeo finished a lap down in fifth position.

Spa Francorchamps (B) May 26
Spa 1000Kms.
Epstein/Liddell Q:12/R:10

In Gardner's hands, a solitary Ford F3L was the class of the field in practice at Francorchamps, Porsche finding its low drag 908 unstable and consequently reverting from long to short tail trim. Porsche had two 908s backed by a 907 while JWA had two GT40s, as usual. Alfa Romeo abstained but Alpine Renault was out again, and Matra brought out a 3.0 litre coupe but neither French car was competitive, nor was a British 3.0 litre Repco-Marcos coupe. The F3L was run closest by Ickx' GT40 while the private GT40 of Mairesse and Blaton was next up, ahead of the 908s.

The combination of Epstein/Liddell was not competitive and the sole T70 representative did not feature, either in practice or in the wet race. Nevertheless, after racing other amateurs and meeting various troubles including low oil pressure the car finished tenth, completing 62 of 71 laps. Ickx/Redman were the easy victors. The 3.0 litre Ford initiated the chase only to start drowning during the first lap, then a challenge by Elford's 908 was stopped by a broken throttle linkage. However, Porsche brought two cars home ahead of the second JWA entry, these two teams again overshadowing the rest of the field.

Watkins Glen (USA) July 14
Watkins Glen Grand Prix (6 Hours)
Bonnier/Axelsson .... Q:6 /R:10

Le Mans should have preceded this trip to the USA but French political and social unrest had postponed the classic at short notice to September. Nevertheless, European entries were thin on the ground at Watkins Glen, though Porsche sent four 908s. In opposition JWA fielded its regular pair of GT40s, now running full 5.0 litre engines, this modification having been recently homologated, while the Bonnier T70 and John Woolfe's unique 3.0 litre Repco-Chevron were the only other tourists. However, the Howmet

Diary continues on page 70

68

car buyer, but Le Mans had worldwide charisma. On paper the old fashioned GT40 was an unlikely winner in '68. In '67 JWA had trimmed its weight and improved its aerodynamics with its so called Mirage version which had featured a slimmer superstructure for a lower frontal area. Working within the freedom of Group 6, the Mirage had still weighed in at over 1000kg. For '68 JWA had to revert to the original heavy GT40 specification, homologated at 4.7 litres though mid season the 5.0 litre version of the Ford V8 was accepted, this taking power from around 400b.h.p. to something in excess of 425b.h.p. using very effective Gurney-Weslake aluminium heads.

Although the car was grossly overweight and aerodynamically inefficient, the Fairlane engine was proven over four seasons as dependable even on 100/102 octane fuel, while the chassis was built like a tank. With superb preparation by the highly professional JWA operation, the GT40 rumbled to victory after victory including Le Mans as the Lola effort came to little and the fleet Porsche prototypes fell by the wayside time and

Jackie Epstein's car is pictured here at Francorchamps and on the previous page at Le Mans, both circuits well suited to the Small Block-Coupe. Alas, this example lacked top line drivers at both World Championship rounds and ran into trouble each time.

again.

The Porsche 3.0 litre engine was based on the marque's road going 911 six cylinder boxer rather than the more complex 2.2 litre eight which was directly descended from an early Sixties Formula One engine. However, unlike the six, it had twin overhead camshafts, though only two valves per cylinder since four valves would not have left room for cooling air to circulate. Porsche continued to champion fan cooling and saw its new 908 boxer as the basis of a future production model.

Whereas the 2.2 litre eight had gear driven camshafts and and overhead fan, the new 908 had chain drive and a vertical fan (VW Beetle style). It was run as two four cylinder engines to the benefit of exhaust tuning potential but this left secondary forces out of balance and severe vibration affected the whole unit leading directly to the retirements of both cars on its debut at Monza.

However, parts were duly reinforced and the 908 won its second race at the Nurburgring. The firing order was subsequently changed yet, though

team was back, with two cars.

Only the Ickx/Bianchi GT40 was quick enough to qualify among the Porsches, taking second on the grid while Bonnier was ahead of Hawkins/ Hobbs and the turbine cars, 2.2 seconds off the pole time. Nevertheless, the early stages of the race found him behind Thompson's turbine. He passed Thompson, then two Porsches ran into trouble elevating him to fourth at the half hour mark, 20 seconds down on the third placed 908 as Ickx led the race half a minute ahead.

Before the one hour mark Porsche found further trouble and soon all four team cars were in the pits for attention to wheel bearings. That left the Lola sandwiched by the JWA team but Bonnier soon lost all but fifth gear and fell far back. JWA was left a straightforward win while Howmet won the prototype class. Having co-opted former US Champion Chuck Parsons to co-drive, Bonnier managed 240 laps to the 286 of the winner to be classified tenth overall.

Zeltweg (A) August 25
Austrian Grand Prix (500Kms.)
Bonnier .... Q:5 /R:NR
de Udy .... Q:8 /R:NR

Run on the Zeltweg airfield circuit, the half distance Austrian World Championship race offered only half the usual points allocation. Nevertheless, Porsche wheeled out four 908s, unopposed by JWA which couldn't improve its points score. The chief opposition came from the Bonnier and de Udy T70s and the now 5.0 litre engined private GT40 of Hawkins. However, a lone Alpine proved surprisingly competitive in prac-

tice, Bianchi joining the three quickest Porsches on the front row, a tenth quicker than Bonnier who was now running a fuel injected engine. Bonnier in turn was three tenths quicker than Hawkins, in spite of being under-geared.

De Udy's practice was spoiled by oil pump drive failure and the same thing sidelined him at the start. Bianchi made the best start but on the first lap all four Porsches and Bonnier overtook the Alpine and Bonnier then overtook the quicker-starting fourth placed Porsche. Although Bonnier found himself unable to attack the other Porsches ahead, it was not long before their number became two. However, at quarter distance Bonnier lay almost a minute behind Siffert's leading car and the two 908s left in front were both looking strong.

Towards half distance Bonnier stopped for fuel earlier than expected, losing some ground. Before he had a chance to regain third place his fuel tank was found to be split, forcing withdrawal of the car. Thus, Hawkins finished third to the 908s.

Le Mans (F) September 29
24 Heures du Mans
Epstein/Nelson Q:16/R:NR
Norinder/Axelsson Q:12/R:NR

The ACO accepted only two T70 entries for its postponed 24 Hour race, both the Epstein and Norinder cars running carburettor engines. Group 4 also contained five GT40s, three 5.0 litre JWA cars plus two 4.7 litre machines, one of which was the Belgian Mairesse/Blaton car that had qualified so well on home ground. In addition there were four 250LMs. In Group 6 four factory 908s were backed by three factory prepared 907s in private hands, all of these brand new cars. Alpine entered four cars, Matra one, all for the glory of France while Woolfe's Repco-Chevron and two Howmet TX turbines completed the 3.0 litre prototype entry.

In practice on Wednesday Norinder suffered an electrical failure but still managed to break the four minute mark.

On Thursday he equalled his 232.0 second clocking, then a valve dropped. That left him 12th on the grid, well away from the 908 215.4 seconds pole time. In contrast the fastest JWA GT40, driven by Rodriguez and Bianchi in the absence of Ickx and Redman, clocked 219.8 seconds and it split the 908s, as did the Matra and the second JWA car driven as usual by Hawkins/Hobbs.

The 908s made the early running, Norinder settling into a position at the bottom of the top ten. Alas, a fuel pick up problem dropped the car down to 20th place, just ahead of the second T70 after the first fuel stops. Later co-driver Axelsson suffered the same fate and he walked further than the permitted 50 metre maximum from the car, so was disqualified. Later on Saturday evening Ed Nelson suffered a puncture on the Epstein car, limping from the Mulsanne to the pits on the wheelrim.

The car came in with the rear body damaged and the engine overheating. It was fixed up and Epstein took over again. Soon after midnight it was found that the car had lost teeth from its final drive pinion. The car restarted after more than three hours work, much of it in the rain. Thus, at 5.00am. it was one of 28 survivors, albeit 70 laps behind the leading GT40 of Rodriguez/Bianchi. The Porsche challenge had crumbled overnight.

Alas, at around 7.30am. the Lola got another puncture, and this time it had to be retired. Cruel luck, indeed. In contrast, the leading JWA 5.0 litre car rumbled on to victory while two delayed Porsches saw the finish in second and third positions. Only one other 3.0 litre Group 6 prototype finished, an Alpine, and only one other Group 4 car finished, the Piper/Attwood 250LM. The result gave Ford the World Championship for Manufacturers with 45 points to the 42 of Porsche. Lola was eighth with one point, taken by Bonnier's car at Brands Hatch.

De Udy's T70 at Sebring '68 goes lawn mowing with a puncture. The car ran as high as third early on, then met trouble...

dampened, the vibration problem persisted to the end of the season due to retention of the (eight pin) flat crank. Porsche entered Le Mans knowing that its alternator faced almost inevitable failure through unavoidable engine vibration...

By this stage the bore had been increased to achieve a full 3.0 litre capacity, engines prior to the Le Mans finale displacing 2.92 litres having inherited bore and stroke dimensions from the 911 series. The 3.0 litre engine was rated 350b.h.p. at a peak power speed of 8,400r.p.m. - 13.8b.h.p. per litre per 1000r.p.m. It was therefore producing considerably less power per revolution than the contemporary Cosworth DFV Formula One engine, which had achieved a figure of 15.0b.h.p. per litre per 1000r.p.m. This was primarily due to its boxer configuration causing high pumping losses.

The 908 had a well designed two valve hemi head which should not have cost it anything in terms of breathing or burning given its modest peak power speed. However, two valves per cylinder did stop it reaching a higher speed without significant loss of volumetric efficiency

and this was another factor in the engine's poor output per litre. A figure of 116b.h.p. per litre was well short of the 142b.h.p. per litre of the DFV, which ran strongly to 9,500r.p.m. with its well designed narrow valve angle pent roof four valve head, producing in total over 425b.h.p.

Nevertheless, the 908 was a quick car by the standards of the 1968 World Championship for Manufacturers. The engine had been slotted into the existing Typ 907 (2.2 litre) g.r.p. bodied spaceframe chassis, with a new six speed gearbox featuring Porsche patent synchromesh the only major chassis alteration, aside from forward shifted fuel tanks to compensate for the additional weight at the rear. The 908 weighed in at 660kg, only 10kg. over the Group 6 minimum and late in the season the introduction of an aluminium rather than steel frame saved 20kg.

The 908 ran on 8" wide front, 12" rear rims and in mid season it was switched to 15" diameter wheels, this allowing it to take advantage of the latest Dunlop Formula One tyres which markedly improved handling. Aerodynamically, the Porsche was conventional with a sloping tail

coupe body notable for a very small low set nose intake (feeding only an oil radiator) and a narrow whale-shaped superstructure. It appeared during the season with nose tabs and with twin flaps in place of the rear spoiler. One flap was to the rear of each wheel arch, higher than the tail and set at a fixed angle, which could be adjusted to vary the downforce obtained.

Porsche wind tunnel tested the 908 during the season, recording a drag co-efficient of Cd Ç 0.422 with the front tabs at 18.5 degrees from the horizontal, the rear flaps at 25 degrees. There was then 44lb. downforce at the front, 140lb. at the rear at a theoretical 300k.p.h. (187.5m.p.h.). Raising the flaps to 35 degrees increased the downforce at the rear to 210lb. with no effect at the front but worsening the drag co-efficient to Cd Ç 0.448. Without the flaps the co-efficient was Cd Ç 0.382 but there was 18lb. lift at the rear. In contrast, the front tabs hardly affected drag, but without them there was 60lb. lift at the front, all these measures at 300k.p.h.

Porsche was not interested in the generation of downforce, merely the mitigation of lift, the minimisation of drag its primary concern. Aside

from its regular body it again produced a long tail for Le Mans. Predictably this reduced stability running in its pure form. In response Porsche devised a clever arrangement of small vertical lateral fins, between which was suspended a tiny aerofoil section incorporating an articulated flap at either end. These flaps were connected to the rear suspension so as to rise and fall as the suspension moved through bump and droop. Tail squat with suspension bump was countered aerodynamically by a corresponding drop of the flap: tail lift in droop was countered by a rise of the flap.

This was perhaps the most interesting aerodynamic development of the '68 sportscar season. Although 1968 was the year of the arrival of the wing in Formula One, with the loss of the Chaparral 2F the high wing no longer featured in the World Championship. Nissan built a T70 lookalike, Chevrolet propelled 5.5 litre Group 6 car and fitted it with a Chaparral-inspired high wing. Ineligible for the World Championship, this machine was not seen outside of Japan. In Japan it was viewed with scepticism, two examples being written off in early testing, one

sadly claiming the life of its driver.

Porsche wind tunnel tested its Le Mans long tailer, with interesting results. With nose tabs and its tail appendage the long tail 908 recorded downforce of 44lb. at the front axle and (with the flaps at 6 degrees) 88lb. at the rear at 300k.p.h. Without the fins and tail assembly no downforce could be achieved at the nose. However, the assembly did not increase drag: the co-efficient was 0.345 with or without the tail appendage. Porsche's tests showed that the rear aerofoil assembly helped keep the flow across the tail attached, this effect countering its own drag.

Porsche started the season with 270b.h.p. from its 2.2 litre engine, then enjoyed an initial 320b.h.p. from the 908. Nevertheless, it could keep up with the JWA GT40s even at Monza thanks to its light weight and low drag. Porsche had already won Daytona and Sebring with the 907 and though it lost Brands Hatch and Monza, it won the Targa Florio with the 907 and the 'Ring and Zeltweg with the 908. Uncharacteristic unreliability let Brands Hatch and Monza slip from its

grasp, the latter not altogether unexpected given the newness of the 908. However, the 908 failed again at Francorchamps, at Watkins Glen and at Le Mans.

The 3.0 litre Porsche made 18 starts during the season but only six times reached the flag without breakage or serious delay. Problems associated with engine vibration were often to blame but the team also suffered a spate of front wheel bearing failures, which also afflicted the 907. All of which left a lot of races to the GT40, a lot more than JWA had dared hope for. JWA did not manage to race-ready its new Group 6 Mirage coupe and that left the team reliant on the GT40 throughout the season, but as Porsche crumbled it won both Le Mans and the World Championship.

The expected challenges from Alpine Renault and Matra came to nought, while Alfa Romeo was not yet ready to show its hand and the Howmet turbine proved little more than an interesting distraction. The most promising of the new Group 6 cars was the Cosworth DFV

ring was Porsche
...us Lola early on,
907 fleet battling the
...0s driven by Scooter
...rick and de Udy, the
...er pictured right.
...ve Siffert's Porsche
...een making the best
...t from pole. The
...0s are fourth (Pa-
...k), ninth (de Udy),
...h (Bonnier) and 34th
...he long line.

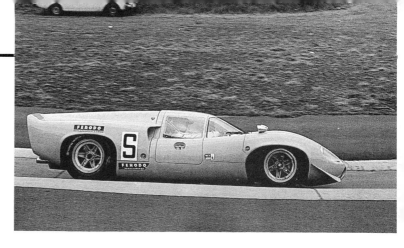

propelled F3L but this lacked development mileage and was only seen at Brands Hatch, Francorchamps and the 'Ring. It was fast but fragile. All of which left the field open to the plodding GT40.

Sure, the T70 was in there pitching, but only on occasion. Newly homologated, the model made its debut as a 5.0 litre Group 4 car at Sebring with a flash of hope as Patrick led at the end of the first hour, and at the end of the second hour. Then the notoriously rough airfield circuit took its toll of his steering. Eventually all four entries fell out, Bonnier finding water in his fuel supply. Never again would the T70 Coupe look so competitive in 1968 World Championship rounds...

Thereafter, only Bonnier of all who drove T70s in World Championship races was a top flight professional driver, and his shoestring effort was not enough to make much of a mark. At Brands Hatch he was soon a lap down on the leading Group 6 2.2 litre Porsche but at least he finished, in sixth place after a flat battery cost better. The less competitive Epstein and Taylor cars retired. Bonnier did not re-appear until the Watkins Glen race; in the meantime the T70 was represented only at the 'Ring and Francorchamps. At the 'Ring Norinder's brand new car (SL73-132) broke its engine after 50 miles, at Francorchamps the Epstein car simply wasn't in contention, this year lacking a top line driver.

Not competitive against the 908s at the Glen, Bonnier got in among them at Zeltweg, only for his fuel tank to split. That was his last Championship race, Le Mans contested by the Epstein and Norinder cars. They were midfield runners bugged by niggling problems.

The 5.0 litre Group 4 version of the T70 Coupe was essentially unchanged from the Chevrolet model seen in '67, though Bonnier played with fuel injection and Broadley introduced a pitched body. This was first seen on the '67 Spyder: the body was canted very slightly forwards, the nose down, tail up attitude slightly increasing downforce.

Away from the World Championship, the T70 did a lot of winning, particularly when run by Sid Taylor who employed some major names. Taylor's car started out winning the Oulton Park Spring Cup in Brian Redman's hands (this post-

Ulf Norinder debuted his T70 at the 'Ring, where Robin Widdows drove with aplomb. Alas, the engine failed early.

BOAC 500 national event contested by the Howmet turbine) then it won the Players' Trophy at Silverstone in Denny Hulme's hands, Hulme pipping Bonnier. Hulme then won the Oulton Park Tourist Trophy after the demise of the pole sitting Ford F3L, then Frank Gardner won the Mallory Park Guards Trophy in the Taylor T70.

At Silverstone in July for the Martini Trophy Sid Taylor brought out a new car, having sold his successful green and white machine to John Woolfe. The new car Hulme drove while Gardner handled the F3L. They had a wonderful scrap until the Ford retired once more. Meanwhile, Bonnier had won the Circuit of Anderstorp in his homeland and soon afterwards de Udy won the Vila Real international in Portugal. Later in the season, de Udy won at Oulton Park after a controversial collision with Bonnier, who had sold his car to David Prophet but had retained use of it to the end of the season.

Earlier, in August the new Taylor car had been given an easy win at Croft by Gardner, then in September Gardner used it to win the Guards Trophy at Brands Hatch, a race which attracted six T70 Coupes, the best turn out of the season. Right at the end of the season Chris Craft gave the Taylor car yet another win, in the poorly supported Circuit of Innsbruck.

Overall, away from World Championship races the T70 Coupe was clearly a highly successful Group 4 car in 1968, easily having the legs of the Ford GT40 and the equally old Ferrari 250LM. Indeed, on a fast circuit such as Silverstone, and in the right hands it was shown to be the equal of a 425b.h.p. Formula One engined, 650kg. Group 6 coupe. But that would not necessarily be the case the following season, when Group 6 cars could be both lighter and smaller...

69

Beetle Game

Having thrown sports car racing into upheaval with its 1968 Groups 4 and 6 capacity limits, during the season the CSI had juggled further with the regulations, reducing the Group 4 homologation quantity for 1969 to 25 units. That decision, made in April '68, meant that Porsche could homologate its 910 Group 6 car of 1967 as a 2.0 litre Group 4 contender, production having already totalled 28 units. Porsche regularly ran fresh chassis and in 1968 it produced a total of 52 cars for its factory team, counting 907 and 908 models.

Aside from that, Porsche was delighted to learn that for '69 Group 6 regulations would be revised with the removal of the 650kg. minimum weight limit and the abolition of the requirements for a proper windscreen and road equipment. Porsche had taken weight reduction to extremes with Group 7 hillclimb cars and was thus perfectly placed to produce an ultra-light Group 6 spyder version of the 908.

While that type of car promised to be highly competitive on most circuits, with a 3.0 litre engine it would not necessarily be a Le Mans winner. Power counted above all at Le Mans: weight saving and drag reduction could not ensure adequate speed on the Mulsanne unless allied to sufficient horsepower from the engine.

Porsche was confined to a two valves per cylinder engine by virtue of its desire to keep its racing relevant to its road car development programme. That meant that the marque could not hope to keep its breathing ability up with increasing engine speed. As 3.0 litre, four valve rivals started to chart territory well above the 8,500r.p.m. seen by the 908 without incurring significant loss of volumetric efficiency, Porsche had to content itself with its existing peak power speed and consequently an inferior output per litre.

Porsche Technical Director Ferdinand Piech wanted to win Le Mans above all else. With rival 3.0 litre cars threatening higher power, the only way was to somehow grasp the sledgehammer. With the cut in the Group 4 homologation quantity Piech won backing from Volkswagen for a 25-off 5.0 litre version of the 908, the Beetle maker keen to see Le Mans won by an air cooled engine. Of course, Piech's grandfather Ferdinand Porsche had designed the Beetle, while his uncle Ferry had founded the Porsche marque with a rebodied Beetle, the heritage of which was the contemporary air cooled six cylinder boxer-engined 911 road car.

The 5.0 litre Typ 917 project was a logical response to the World Championship for Manufacturers capacity limits. And it promised a return to power at a time when Le Mans thought it had checked rising speed. However, at the start of the '69 season it was still secret and not scheduled to debut before May and thus the Lola T70 was still the fastest thing in Group 4. Its degree of competitiveness relative to the pace making Porsche 908 Group 6 car had clearly been affected by the modified Prototype regulations, but at Le Mans and other fast circuits it could hope to hold its own.

However, the re-entry of Ferrari with its contemporary Formula One engine was worrying. That four valve per cylinder V12 ran to 9,800r.p.m. producing 420b.h.p. - a comparable output to that of the 5.0 litre Chevrolet, and an output asked to propelled a car weighing significantly less than 800kg. Further, although the Alan Mann Ford F3L project had apparently died, behind the scenes JWA was still developing its own BRM Formula One engined Group 6 car. Then there were strengthening Group 6 efforts by Alfa Romeo, Alpine and Matra to consider...

The T70 could expect to find it tough in '69 World Championship races, even though Broadley had a revised chassis boasting less weight, brake and suspension modifications and improved aerodynamics - the MK.IIIB. More so since there was still no official works team. Lola Cars' greatest hope was the super-professional Roger Penske Racing Team, which planned to run a Mk.IIIB at Daytona and Sebring.

Pennsylvanian Chevrolet dealer Penske had put together a deal with Lola Cars and its American distributor Carl Haas to run Lolas in USAC, Can Am and Formula A (as well as a Trans Am programme with a Camaro). Penske regularly won the Trans Am Championship with driver/engineer Mark Donohue (twice U.S.R.R.C. winner) and was noted for meticulous preparation.

His operation was the equal of JWA.

In the UK, Sid Taylor was offered works support for a T70 Mk.IIIB and a T142 F5000 (Formula A - UK) car, both these machines utilising the 5.0 litre Small Block Chevrolet engine. These and the T162 Can Am and T150 USAC cars comprised Lola's '69 output, the marque still concentrating on big engined machinery, much of it destined for export. In Europe, Bonnier arranged to handle Lola distribution on the continent from his base in Switzerland, and to run a Mk.IIIB in Europe in conjunction with the Swiss Ecurie Filipinetti. Whereas Taylor planned only selected rounds of the WCM, Bonnier hoped to attack them all, arranging to co-drive Ulf Norinder's Sports Cars Unlimited, Switzerland Mk.IIIB in the season opening US races.

Inside the Slough factory in late '68 - this is the works Can Am T610 from which the '69 T612 Can Am and T70 MkIIIB Coupes derived.

Logical Move

Although homologated into Group 4 on the basis that it was a development of the Mk.III T70, the Mk.IIIB was a new car, with many new parts. It should not be confused with the so called Mk.IIIB Spyder, which had been the marque's '67 works team Can Am challenger and was similar under the skin to the '67 production Coupe and Spyder models. The IIIB Can Am model had continued in '68 as the customer Spyder while Surtees had aired a much more substantially revised works Can Am car, the T160 and it was from this that the Mk.IIIB Coupe was derived, as was the T162 '69 customer Can Am car.

The T160 was a derivative of the T70 series with a lighter yet stiffer all-alloy tub having torsional rigidity quoted as 7,500 lb.ft. per degree, over twice that of the T70 and around three quarters that of the '66 Ford GT40 Mk.II with its weighty reinforced steel tub, and of the honeycomb Mk.IV. Otherwise the car was a logical development of the T70, with some suspension and brake developments. Nevertheless, in prototype form it was not a success for Surtees, Broadley blaming this on lack of development time. Only small modifications were required for the T162 production car, from which the Mk.IIIB coupe was derived.

The monocoque tub was now all aluminium alloy aside from two detachable magnesium cross members incorporated in the roll hoop at the back of the cockpit. Weight was saved wherever possible, the aim to bring the car down to the regulation minimum 800kg. The fuel was carried entirely in the lefthand sponson, balancing the weight of the driver, the righthand sponson carrying only the battery. The fuel - still around 32 gallons - was collected in a rear mounted surge tank that incorporated a non-returnable valve and fuel was pumped to the engine via twin Bendix electric pumps once again.

The LG500 five speed transmission was retained, albeit with redesigned c.w.p. following earlier failures. The wheelbase was unaltered while the suspension was refined with new uprights to assist brake cooling improvements and to suit a choice of rim widths: 8", 10", 11" or 12.5" at the front, 10", 14" and 17" at the rear, the track varying accordingly to a maximum of 57"/1448mm. The rims were of 15" diameter with a 13" option for the rear while the tread width was ever increasing following Formula One development. Typical springs were now in the region of 450lb.

The brakes were now located in a conventional position, within the wheel rim (and outside the uprights front and rear) and cooling air was ducted to them. Girling supplied 1.1" thick radially ventilated 12" diameter cast iron discs and aluminium four pot calipers. Cooling air was collected from the central nose intake, by ducts flanking the radiator each duct feeding a new aluminium casting bolted to the respective front upright. The casting was designed to feed air to the eye of the disc, into the radial ventilation channels. A similar concept was employed at the rear where the feed was taken from periscope-type ducts emerging through the tail.

The body was subtly reshaped, sleeker than before with a drooping nose. Four headlights were now fitted, two behind each perspex fairing while for dry sump engines twin oil coolers were fitted, one in each mid located engine cooling air intake. The gullwing doors were replaced by lighter, arguably safer, forward hinged doors.

Aside from reduced weight and a stiffer chassis, the main feature of the Mk.IIIB Coupe was its aerodynamics. Although superficially it looked the same as the familiar Mk.III Coupe, the nose

*MkIIIB featured
ed aerodynamics,
er set nose intake
bvious modifica-
This is the model
s Daytona debut,
hue at the controls
e very competitive
e-run example. It
the race.*

re-shaping was very significant. In essence, the nose reached further forward so that the radiator intake was lower set. Its bottom lip then became almost a horizontal splitter, cleanly dividing the oncoming air and encouraging the air to flow over the top surface of the nose rather than underneath.

Traditional streamlined sportscar noses were designed to cut through the air as a ship's prow cuts through water, hopefully thereby minimising drag. However, in '67 Chaparral and Ford had introduced the concept of discouraging air from flowing under the hull. This was found to reduce lift by mitigating the significant lifting

effect caused by air packing under the nose. At the same time it reduced drag since there was less ground shear effect when less air flowed under the car.

The Mk.IIIB did not get a slab sided body but its modified nose reduced the underbody airflow flow and created significantly more pressure on its upper surface. Increased downforce at the front of the Mk.IIIB was matched by a prominent rear spoiler which was significantly wider than seen before. The Mk.IIIB was homologated at the minimum 800kg. carrying a Small Block Chevrolet and the first car weighed in at 860kg. with oil and water on board.

Daytona (USA) February 1

Daytona 24 Hours

Donohue/Parsons .... Q: 2/R:1
Bonnier/Norinder .... Q: 5/R:NR
Patrick/Jordan Q:10/R:7
Motschenbacher/Leslie Q:11/R:2

Roger Penske had thoroughly rebuilt his new T70 Mk.IIIB, replacing parts where he deemed strengthening necessary for 24 hour longevity, and it was clear that in the hands of American road racing stars Mark Donohue and Ronnie Bucknum the car was a very serious threat to the establishment. The establishment, of course, being Porsche and JWA, the former having five familiar 908s, the latter two familiar, '68 World Championship winning GT40s with full 5.0 litre engines.

The Lola challenge was backed up by Ulf Norinder's Sports Cars Unlimited Team and James Garner's AIR team. Sharing with Bonnier, Norinder had a Mk.IIIB with a carburettor engine whereas Penske used fuel injection. The AIR machines were older cars running carburettor engines and their drivers had, of course, been in the actor's squad on its last World Championship appearance at Sebring in '68, aside that is from Lothar Motschenbacher, a Can Am regular.

Practice knocked out the only other serious entry, a 3.0 litre Matra coupe while Bucknum found a finger broken in a motorcycle accident giving him trouble and he was replaced by Chuck Parsons. Meanwhile, Donohue lapped in 112.7 seconds which was beaten only by one other car, the 908 of Vic Elford and Redman which went 112.2 seconds. Two other Porsches got ahead of Bonnier/Norinder while the faster Ickx/Jacky Oliver JWA GT40 clocked 114.5 seconds,

slower than all five Porsches.

Elford took the initiative at the start, leading Siffert's 908, Donohue and Bonnier around the first lap. The second lap saw Siffert swoop into the lead running higher on the banking, then the two Lolas took turns at leading. After 45 minutes all but nine cars had been lapped, these nine the four leaders, the three other Porsches and the JWA Fords chasing them. However, the second GT40 was close to being lapped by the leading quartet.

Alas, the well placed Lolas hit trouble before the first hour was up. First Donohue found a fuel pick up problem and chugged to the pits, then Bonnier came in with nose damage having been pincered by two slow tailenders. Thus Porsche was left filling the first five positions, tracked doggedly by the JWA cars with the AIR cars rumbling along a lap or so behind. Worse befell the Bonnier/Norinder car in the second hour, Norinder hitting the wall of the banking as he swerved to avoid a slower car. Damage to the right rear corner proved beyond repair.

After three hours the Porsche parade started crumbling. Redman suffered a cracked exhaust that took 20 minutes to fix and before the job was finished another 908 came in with the same trouble. Then a third and a fourth car were affected and JWA was starting to look a better bet. However, at the six hour mark 908s were holding first and second positions, the leader still with its original exhaust system and four laps up on the GT40s, five laps up on the Penske car in fifth place. The three other 908s were split by Jordan/Patrick who were 11 laps down on the leader.

Although having to run on effectively two thirds of a tank, the Penske T70 was well in contention but after seven and a half hours Donohue stopped with his exhaust badly cracked. The entire system had to be removed, patched up and replaced and the job took 79 minutes, losing the car over 40 laps. Nevertheless, it plugged on gamely.

Just after nine hours running, the

leading 908's engine failed. Soon another Porsche engine failed, for the same reason: a breakage in the gear-based valve drivetrain. Progressively, the other German cars fell out as night gave way to day.

At 9.00am, 18 hours into the race, just one 908 held sway at the front of the field and JWA had now lost one car, again to engine failure. The upshot was that the Penske T70 held third overall, albeit way, way back from the leaders, while the Motschenbacher/Leslie car was even further back, behind various club racing machines in tenth overall. Now the better placed of the troubled AIR team's cars, it had suffered overheating due to a radiator blockage. The only solution had been a complete change of radiator.

Almost inevitably the leading Porsche eventually succumbed to valve train failure but surprisingly the Ickx/Oliver GT40 also retired, Ickx crashing at the exit from the banking. Thus, Donohue/Parsons were left at the front of a motley collection of amateur-run production cars, through which the Motschenbacher/Leslie T70 was cutting a path. It took over an hour for Donohue/Parsons to unwind the advantage of the parked JWA car, but the Penske Lola was running like a train. So was the Motschenbacher/Leslie machine and with two hours to run it had also regained lost ground: Chevrolet Lolas lay first and second. Both made it home, the leading car 30 laps ahead.

Sebring (USA) March 22

Sebring 12 Hours

Donohue/Bucknum .... Q: 2/R:NR
Bonnier/Norinder .... Q: 7/R:NR
Patrick/Jordan .... Q: 5/R:NR
Motschenbacher/Leslie ...... Q: 6/R:6

The serious runners at Sebring were those seen at Daytona plus a major new challenge from Italy. Of the key 11 Daytona contestants, Porsche had switched to

Diary continues on page 82

On a Shoestring

In February 1969 the Lola T70 Coupe took its one and only World Championship win. The following month it saw its end in view. Its inevitable fate was to be slaughtered by a potent new 5.0 litre Group 4 car propelled by a full race engine. Porsche unveiled this at the Geneva Motor Show in March 1969.

Porsche had spared no expense on its Typ 917 programme. Zuffenhausen's 25-off Sports-Prototype was based on a brand new engine which, while still air cooled and thus logically of 'flat' configuration was a 180 degree V12 rather than the seemingly inevitable boxer. With opposite pistons sharing a crankpin rather than moving towards each other, losses through pumping and windage were drastically reduced. Consequently, torque increased, even if the established 908 peak power speed could not be beneficially raised due to the retention of two valves per cylinder.

The existing Chevrolet and Ford wedge head pushrod engines used in Group 4 were capable of running only to 7,000r.p.m. due to valve train inertia constraints while producing in the region of 12.5 b.h.p. per litre per 1000r.p.m. on the regulation 100/102 octane fuel. The main drawback in that respect was the old fashioned wedge head. The contemporary Cosworth DFV Formula One engine was capable of producing 15.0 b.h.p. per litre per 1000r.p.m. on the same

spyder body and had five of its brand new 908/2s, with engine modified to help overcome the Daytona vibration-related exhaust and valve train problems. The modified engine had a flat plane crankshaft: given the 180 degree configuration of the Stuttgart eight cylinder boxer, this resulted in full secondary balance, hence smoother running.

JWA had reverted from 'dry deck' to proven 'wet deck' 5.0 litre V8s for its two GT40s following the Daytona engine failure, traced to the re-routing of the coolant flow from block to head. Meanwhile, Penske had switched from fuel injection to carburettors. Otherwise the four car Lola force was as seen at Daytona, with Bucknum back in the seat of the Sunoco blue Mk.IIIB.

The fresh Italian challenge consisted of three 3.0 litre V8 T33-3s from Alfa Romeo's Autodelta competition wing and a lone, similarly brand new Ferrari 60 degree V12 3.0 litre 312P. Both Italian marques were running their Group 6 cars as spyders (and still non of the contestants were using wings).

In testing prior to the event Donohue was fastest, clocking 161.8 seconds. Fastest of the 15 leading runners in first practice was the Mitter 908 which did 162.7 seconds with Siffert two tenths slower. However, after adjustment to a troublesome gear linkage, the following day Chris Amon went out in the Ferrari and clocked 160.4 seconds for pole.

Donohue responded with 160.9 seconds, one tenth faster than Amon's co-driver Mario Andretti. The two quickest Porsches kept their Thursday times for third and fourth grid positions, then came the three other Lolas, Patrick/Jordan clocking 163.4 for fifth position.

The quickest Alfa Romeo did 165.6 seconds, the quickest GT40, 167.4 seconds which was only good enough for 12th position.

At the off the 312P did not promptly respond to Amon's command: Siffert led the first lap with Donohue in among the Porsches in fourth place, the Ferrari seventh. Siffert continued to lead the race until the first round of fuel stops as Elford's 908 suffered a damaged corner. Amon and Donohue mixed with the three other 908s running in Siffert's wake and the Lola took over the lead when Siffert refuelled. Having run ten laps longer than the 908, Bucknum took the T70 out in second place, again chasing the Siffert/Redman car, now driven by the latter, and in turn chased by Amon.

Already the Alfa Romeo challenge had crumbled, while the Patrick Lola had suffered terminal overheating. Towards quarter distance Redman needed an eight minute stop to repair a damaged steering arm, letting the Lola back into the lead. However, the Ferrari soon forged ahead, as did the Gerhard Mitter/Udo Schutz 908. Soon afterwards the Bonnier/Norinder Lola retired with a broken suspension mount. Half an hour or so later the Penske T70 retired from third place for the same reason.

The leading Ferrari and Porsche continued to battle through the half distance mark, by which stage JWA had lost its Hobbs/Mike Hailwood car to suspension failure and Porsche had lost two cars, each to a similar frame fracture. AIR still had one car running, in fifth place, behind the Ferrari, two Porsches and the Ickx/Oliver GT40 and nine laps down on the leader. The lead battle broke up early in the second half of the race when the Ferrari collected nose damage that affected its cooling system.

At the eight and a half hour mark the leading 908 was hit by frame fracture. Repair was attempted; this took over half an hour. That left the ailing Ferrari ahead of the only untroubled 908, the Ickx/Oliver GT40 and the AIR T70. With the

Porsche seemingly destined for frame fracture and the Ferrari limping the T70 looked set for second. Alas, AIR suffered a wheel bearing failure and finished 10 laps behind in fifth place as the GT40 beat the sick Ferrari and a trio of Porsches, one a privately entered 907, the others patched up 908s.

Le Mans (F) April 13
Le Mans Test Weekend

On March 12, at the Geneva Motor Show Press Day, Porsche had startled the motoring world with its 4.5 litre Typ 917 Group 4 coupe. Where the existing 5.0 litre Ford and Lola Group 4 cars had pushrod engines producing in the region of 450b.h.p. the new Porsche had a full race engine with an official 520b.h.p. In fact, as the car was seen at the Test Weekend, engine creator Hans Mezger subsequently confirmed to the author it had the best part of 550b.h.p at its disposal, with more to come.

Such performance made the two factory fresh examples at Le Mans the centre of attention. However, no previous running had been done outside the confines of the factory grounds and at speed on the Mulsanne the car proved almost undriveable, weaving all over the road. Consequently, the drivers could not explore the full potential of the engine: 199m.p.h. was run using restricted r.p.m. That was good enough for a 210.7 second lap - the best part of five seconds inside Siffert's '68 908 pole time.

Overshadowed, Lola Cars had a brand new T70 coupe, which Hawkins drove. The nose grounded and required patching up and the engine would not pull strongly, leaving the car short of speed on the Mulsanne. A best lap of 215.2 seconds was recorded.

JWA did not attend the test so there was no other Group 4 yardstick for the 917. In Group 6, Ferrari and Matra put in quick laps, the Sebring 312P spyder

Diary continues on page 84

fuel while running to 9,500r.p.m. A well designed pent roof, shallow valve angle four valve head allowed the DFV to soar past the 8,400r.p.m. level of the Porsche 908 engine while maintaining a higher level of power per litre per 1000r.p.m. than either the American engines or the hemi head German contender.

Meanwhile, with its Boxer configuration the twin cam 908 engine gave a comparatively low 13.8b.h.p. per litre per 1000r.p.m. in spite of a well designed hemi head and its relatively easy-breathing peak power speed of 8,400r.p.m. Porsche knew that, given two valves per cylinder, it could not climb to higher revolutions without significant loss of volumetric efficiency but in rejecting the inefficient boxer configuration it sought a solid 15.0b.h.p. per litre per 1000r.p.m. from its new 5.0 litre weapon at its existing modest speed level.

In fact, Porsche started out with only 4.5 litres, retaining the cylinder dimensions of its 908 engine for logistical reasons while slightly modifying the shape of the combustion chamber for higher efficiency. Nevertheless, if it could achieve the target 15.0b.h.p. per litre per 1000r.p.m. of the DFV it would have a solid 567b.h.p. at 8,400r.p.m. - a massive advance over the existing pushrod, wedge head Group 4 engines and enough horsepower to make a higher speed 3.0 litre Formula One engine look pale.

The 917 engine started life with a test bed reading of almost 550b.h.p, its creator Hans Mezger later informed the author. By the time

of the 1969 Le Mans race it was pumping out 565b.h.p. at 8,400r.p.m. Clearly, the 5.0 litre Chevrolet and Ford V8s were history.

But the T70 Coupe had one last fling. It had always been in its element at Francorchamps and in Mk.IIIB trim it found equal empathy with the new Osterreichring. That was again a tribute to its solid chassis technology - fully exploiting the ever improving tyres - and, more importantly, to its aerodynamics. Its mechanical grip was good and in Mk.IIIB trim its aerodynamic grip was better than ever.

Once the overheating dramas that plagued the model at Brands Hatch had been sorted, the Mk.IIIB's low droop nose was a complete suc-

'70 rivals in '69 included the powerful new Porsche 917 (below) the Ferrari 12P spyder, the Porsche 908/2 spyder and the Ford GT40. The new 917 is seen at the 'Ring, the two spyders are pictured together at Brands Hatch while the JWA GT40 is running ahead of the Penske T70 at Daytona. The Penske team was the equal of JWA but did not contest the European races.

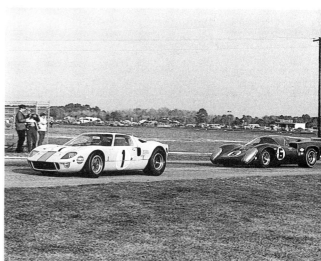

running 217.8 seconds, the latest spyder version of the 3.0 litre V12 propelled Matra 630/650 running 213.9 seconds. Less impressive times were clocked by Alpine and Alfa Romeo. Alpine had two '68 coupes awaiting improved engines while Alfa Romeo ran a Sebring spyder. Bianchi was killed when this car crashed on the Mulsanne.

Brands Hatch (GB) April 13
BOAC 500 (6 Hours)

Bonnier/Muller	*Q:19/R:20*
Widdows/Norinder	*Q:21/R:21*
Revson/Axelsson/Hulme	*Q: 8/R:NR*
Craft/Liddell	*Q: 9/R:8*
Piper/Pierpoint	*Q:11/R:17*
Taylor/Dibley	*Q:15/R:19*
Prophet/Nelson	*Q:16/R:NR*
Hawkins/Williams	*Q: 6/R:NR*

No less than eight T70s assembled for the Brands Hatch six hour race, half a dozen of which were in Mk.IIIB trim. Only one of the teams - Norinder's Sportscar Unlimited - had been seen in the USA. Group 4 opposition was headed by the JWA GT40 of Hobbs/Hailwood, in addition to which the class contained three amateur-run examples. JWA had put its lead pairing of Ickx/Oliver in its new 3.0 litre BRM-Mirage coupe. In Group 6 this new challenger faced a new Ferrari 312P spyder (to Sebring specification) and four Porsche 908/2 spyders, these having strengthened chassis frames. The other serious runner in Group 6 was the Alan Mann Ford F3L.

Siffert and Amon were quickest in qualifying, the Group 4 runners overshadowed by the new generation lightweight spyders on this tight track. On race day Amon pressured Siffert for a little over than half an hour, then suffered a puncture. The way was then open for a Porsche parade. At one stage during the demonstration of renewed Stuttgart reliability it looked as though the Ferrari might recover sufficiently to penetrate high among the Porsche ranks but a stretched throttle cable put paid to that. However, one 908/2 hit crash debris and dropped to sixth, leaving Porsche a one - two - three finish.

The 312P came home fourth, by less than 30 seconds, while the JWA GT40 rumbled home fifth. Out of serious contention for victory, the Group 4 leader at the end of the first hour had been the Hawkins/Jonathan Williams T70, sixth overall but a lap down. Nevertheless, it led the disappointing Mirage and Ford F3L Group 6 prototypes, both of which subsequently fell out. Craft/Liddell and Pierpoint/Piper had been well in contention, while the GT40 had been set back by an early stop to rectify a fuel leak.

The JWA Group 4 challenge had emerged in the third hour, Hobbs/Hailwood then lying third in class to Hawkins/Williams and Pierpoint/Piper, Craft/Liddell suffering a minor setback. After three hours 50 minutes running the Hawkins/Williams Lola broke a rear wishbone and that had let JWA into the class lead, which it retained to the finish. Meanwhile, the Mk.IIIBs suffered widespread overheating dramas to the extent that the older Craft/Liddell Tech-Speed car was left upholding the honour of the marque. It finished two laps down to the GT40, in eighth overall.

Prophet/Nelson had posted Lola's first retirement, after only four laps due to an oil leak. The first car to succumb to overheating was that of Peter Revson/Axelsson who had been joined by F3L pilot Hulme. This car was also in brake trouble. Taylor/Dibley's Team Elite car had been high up in the opening laps but had gradually slowed. Eventually, they and Piper/Pierpoint (in the former's car) had to withdraw, though both cars covered enough distance to be classified, as did the Bonnier/Muller machine.

Frustrated by overheating delays, towards the end of the race Bonnier took over the Scuderia Filipinetti car from Herbie Muller and started charging along, bumping the Hobbs/Hailwood GT40 then crashing out at Bottom Bend with a spectacular somersault!

Monza (I) April 25
1000Km. di Monza

Gardner/de Adamich	*Q: 9/R:5*
Bonnier/Muller	*Q: 7/R:NR*
Craft/Liddell	*Q:15/R:NR*
Piper/Hawkins	*Q:14/R:NR*
Norinder/Widdows	*Q:10/R:NR*

In spite of the speed of the Monza autodrome, the Group 6 prototypes from Porsche and Ferrari headed qualifying, Andretti taking pole ahead of Siffert and Rodriguez in a second 312P spyder. Porsche was running its 908 coupe once again and had a total of four cars sporting long tails. The three other 908s were split by Johnny Servoz-Gavin in the Matra spyder seen at the test weekend, and Bonnier in the quickest Group 4 car. Behind Bonnier's yellow Filipinetti car, the fifth row of the grid contained Gardner in Taylor's car and Widdows in Norinder's machine. Further back were of pair of Alpine coupes but no sign of the works Alfa Romeos or the JWA team.

The first lap saw the Ferrari, Porsche and Matra prototypes break away from the rest of the field, the rumbling T70 simply not fleet enough. Worse, Bonnier, Gardner and Widdows all pitted on the first lap, Bonnier already facing terminal engine trouble while incidents in the heavy traffic had set the other cars back. The upshot was that as the race settled down, the Group 4 contest was led by the privately entered Ford GT40 of Germans Hans Kelleners/Reinhold Joest. This car was chased by the T70s of Piper and Craft and within 150 kilometres a

Diary continues on page 86

cess and the car's high speed cornering was superb and was the envy of Porsche. At the Osterreichring it was the 917's inferior aerodynamics which left it to be mercilessly monstered by Bonnier's low budget T70, in spite of its huge 25% power advantage.

Bonnier's splendid second place at the Osterreichring was a fitting tribute to the excellence of the T70 Mk.IIIB Coupe. An excellence which was underlined by Porsche's long struggle to make the 917 raceworthy.

Just as the 908 had essentially been a 907 with a new, larger engine and a new, stronger transmission, so the 917 was essentially a 908 with a new, larger engine and a new, stronger transmission. The two long tail versions taken to the Le Mans test weekend ran the Mulsanne at almost 200m.p.h. but weaved all over the Route Nationale, to the extent that full throttle could not be applied. Fitted with a short tail, the model weaved even more alarmingly.

Since in its early guise the 908 had been more stable through Francorchamp's sweeping bends in short tail than in long tail trim, the example

raced in the Spa 1000Kms. was in short tail trim, with nose tabs and rear flaps, the latter articulated and responding to suspension movement as had those on the 908 Le Mans car. Nevertheless, Porsche admitted that the car: "was quite unstable and dangerous in the fast bends of Spa... and did not behave much better on the straight". Quite a contrast to the behaviour of the equally potent 5.9 litre T70 Coupe on its debut at Francorchamps two years previously...

Siffert took pole from Hawkins' 5.0 litre, 440b.h.p. T70 Coupe by a mere 0.6 second, in spite of his massive power advantage - and elected to race a slower 908. For Le Mans the car was set up with a slight forward pitch - just half a degree - and this improved stability, allowing it to be run flat out on the Mulsanne. Steeper front tabs and modification to the rear flap linkage for a higher average angle of attack also helped.

Nevertheless, running an estimated 215m.p.h. - roughly the speed of the Mk.IVs in '67 - the car still required a lot of road and was a real handful through the kink. None of the hands off stability

e Bonnier T70 kIIIB leads the Tay-example at Monza, rdner in the latter . These, the quick-of a five-strong 0 fleet did not have legs of the Porsche d Ferrari 3.0 litre rks cars.

the 5.0 litre machines had been lapped.

Piper's car moved up to challenge the German GT40 before the first fuel stops, at which Hawkins relieved him while Liddell took over from Craft. Alas, Hawkins suffered a front wheel bearing seizure, then Liddell heard rumblings from the transmission. Both these cars were for retirement, as was the delayed Widdows/Norinder machine, which likewise suffered transmission failure.

By one third distance the Taylor Lola had come back into contention, running on the same lap as the class leading German GT40 which was in seventh overall thanks to the retirement of one Porsche. By half distance the Amon/Andretti Ferrari had retired with engine failure and not long afterwards the second Ferrari crashed at very high speed when it lost its rear bodywork, a tail fixing having been damaged in an earlier incident.

The demise of Ferrari left Porsche unchallenged for the first three positions after a hectic dog fight. Fourth place was now disputed between the Group 4 leaders, a 2.5 litre Alfa Romeo T33 run by Team VDS, a surviving Alpine and a private 2.0 litre Porsche 910. Running like clockwork, the 910 moved to the front of the queue and found itself third overall as a 908 crashed out, victim of tyre failure. The VDS car hit trouble, leaving the Lola to fight the German Ford and the Alpine for fourth place.

As the winning 908 completed its final lap the German GT40 was fending off the Alpine, both cars in turn being caught by Gardner in the Lola. As the trio left the Lesmo corners there was a mix up and Gardner hit the rear of the Alpine which went careering off the course. Thrown by this incident, Gardner narrowly failed to beat the GT40, which thus claimed class honours.

Cefalu (I) May 4
Targa Florio (720Km.)
Bonnier/Muller .... R:NR

Although the brutish T70 looked far from its element on the 44 mile long Little Madonie rally-style mountain course, Scuderia Filipinetti/Bonnier sportingly ran this unusual round of the World Championship for Manufacturers. Unsurprisingly, the T70 was the only large capacity entry in Group 4. The event was logically Porsche versus Alfa Romeo, with seven factory entries of Group 6 prototypes, though only one of them from Italy. Ferrari abstained but Autodelta came out with a 2.5 litre T33 for Nino Vaccarella and Andrea de Adamich. Naturally, the factory Porsches were all 908/2 models, and all were brand new chassis.

Muller had trouble getting the Lola away at the start, losing a couple of minutes. Nevertheless, he passed car after car on the first lap, clocking a splendid 2233.1 seconds lap (only 70.8 seconds from the lap record) to run third overall. Alas, he picked up a flat tyre on the second lap. Thankfully running on the rim didn't put the car out. Meanwhile, a much more nimble 2.0 litre Alfa Romeo T33 driven with gusto by Nanni Galli had taken over the Group 4 lead. It similarly was lying well up among the Porsches, only to get punted out by Elford's 908/2! The 2.5 litre Autodelta car also retired, and Bonnier lost a wheel on the long straight by the sea, leaving Porsche a clean sweep of the top four positions.

Francorchamps (B) May 11
1000Km. de Spa-Francorchamps
Bonnier/Muller Q:4/R:5
Hawkins/Prophet Q:1/R:8
Troberg/Rothstein Q:18/R:11

With its emphasis upon power, grip and high speed handling, the Francorchamps circuit was one at which the T70 was always very much at home, whereas the new Porsche 917 was found to be at sea. The Stuttgart transporter unloaded two of the recently homologated 4.5 litre Group 4 coupes as back ups to the 908s driven by star pairings Siffert/Redman and Elford/Ahrens. Siffert took one around in 221.9 seconds for pole position but that was an act of great bravery. The new machine was dangerously unstable. Thus, Siffert elected to drive a 908 coupe, though Mitter agreed to race the beast.

Siffert's decision left pole position to Hawkins who had lapped in 221.3 seconds in spite of a plus-100b.h.p. deficit compared to the 917. Running on home ground, Ickx was second fastest in the hitherto troublesome 3.0 litre BRM-Mirage coupe. Siffert took the outside of the front row with a time of 228.6 seconds, then came Bonnier and the 312P which Rodriguez was sharing with Piper, while the three other works Porsches were on the third row, the 917 to the outside.

Further back, JWA had a second Mirage coupe rather than a GT40 and Alpine had three coupes to complete the factory entries. In Group 4, aside from three T70s, there were two GT40s including the Joest/Kelleners machine that ran so well at Monza. The class lost its new Porsche right at the start, Mitter contriving both to ruin the clutch and over-rev the engine. Meanwhile, Hawkins made the best start to lead the first lap with Siffert, Rodriguez and Ickx on his heels. After a couple of laps Siffert and Rodriguez demoted Hawkins while Ickx dropped away.

Bonnier stopped early with a loose plug lead but Hawkins kept up with the two leading Group 6 cars. On lap eight of 71 Rodriguez brushed a slower car, this forcing the Ferrari into the pits for a checkover of its bodywork. Hawkins continued to run in Siffert's wheeltracks and when the Porsche stopped for fuel after an hour of racing, the Lola had another lap in the lead.

Diary continues on page 88

where near so well as the spyder.

The first step was fitting a nose with an air dam prow below the small radiator inlet: this brought immediate improvement and made it even more evident that rear downforce was missing. JWA had been invited along to the test since it had agreed to run the works Porsche team in 1970. JWA Chief Engineer John Horsman noted from the pattern of splattered gnats on the bodywork that the airstream appeared to be shooting right over the rear flaps. Horsman and his Crew Chief Ermanno Cuoghi came up with the idea of trying a high rear deck, one that reflected the lines of the Can Am spyder.

Right from the outset the 917 had been designed for low drag and that implied a whale-shaped superstructure. Porsche knew that its 5.0 litre 25-off challenger would be followed by a similar machine from Ferrari: that car would have state of the art four valve heads. Thus, it would run to a higher speed without significant loss of breathing or combustion efficiency and in so doing would take power beyond Porsche's reach. With that in mind, the 917 had been designed to keep right on the 800kg. minimum weight limit and to enjoy the minimum of drag.

To fit the high deck improvised by Cuoghi was a major challenge to Porsche philosophy. Yet, in the circumstances it was the obvious fix to try... and it worked. With the higher downforce nose and the new tail, driver Kurt Ahrens reported: "very good, very stable. Good road-holding and good stability in the turns".

Porsche Technical Director Ferdinand Piech

Bonnier at Francorchamps: fourth on the grid, the car suffered a loose plug lead on the very first lap. It finished a distant fifth after a number of other adventures.

Overheating dramas plagued the T70 MkIIIBs at Brands Hatch. This is Sid Taylor's works-supported example...

of the big Fords. A lot lighter than the Ford Mk.IV, though, the 917 accelerated faster and could brake later. Over the entire lap it was a little quicker (allowing for the installation of a chicane just before the pits). With a slightly inferior dry weight and a far lower power level the higher drag T70 could not compete.

Then came the Osterreichring race. The 917 once again ran in short tail trim, with front tabs and the rear flaps, these now fixed thanks to a regulation change and set at a high angle. The drivers still didn't much like the car, particularly the way it oversteered around the blind righthander at the top of the hill past the pits. Nevertheless, Siffert drove the difficult beast to victory...just.

Much better handling was enjoyed by a Can Am spyder version of the 917 run at the same circuit in testing a couple of months later. The Can Am car ran alongside the coupe, the latter still in short tail trim and with stiffer springs to reduce pitch changes. Nevertheless, the flaps had to be set vertical and the car handled no-

Whereas Porsche and Ferrari were refuelling using pressure hoses, the Lola crew had only churns and as a result Hawkins dropped back behind Rodriguez who had lost very little time to his unscheduled stop. Ahrens' 908 was now fourth, Ickx having met trouble, and it came up to catch and pass the Lola during the second hour. Hawkins then handed over to the slower David Prophet and while Siffert/Redman and Elford/Ahrens raced Rodriguez/Piper, the Lola ran steadily in fourth place. Alas, engine failure with less than 100kms. to run dropped the car to eighth. Bonnier then won Group 4 in fifth overall after a troubled run while the Ferrari ended as the meat in a Porsche sandwich.

Nurburgring (D) June 1
ADAC 1000Kms.
Bonnier/Muller .... Q: 5/R:NR
Prophet/Nelson Q:11/R:NR
Troberg/Rothstein .... Withdrew

If the T70 was a handful at the 'Ring thanks to its size and weight compared to the Group 6 spyders, the 917 was almost unmanageable. Porsche brought just one example and all its drivers wanted to stay with the far faster 908/2 model. In one of these Siffert did a lap within a tenth of a second of the magic eight minute barrier, a feat matched by Amon who was back in the 312P. Meanwhile, Bonnier led Group 4 with a lap around half a minute slower while the engine of the Prophet/Nelson car kept seizing.

With two factory-prepared cars run by the Porsche Salzburg team, Porsche had six spyders against the lone Ferrari spyder of Amon/Rodriguez. Also in Group 6, JWA brought out two revised Mirage coupes, one with a Cosworth DFV, the other with a stronger 48 rather than 24 valve example of the BRM V12 engine. However, neither version worked well on the long mountain circuit. In Group 4 the Kelleners/Joest GT40 was again present while the T70 representation was reduced to two cars when Rothstein crashed heavily. However, the 917 ran, driven carefully by Piper and Gardner.

The German crewed GT40 made all the running on race day, Bonnier in trouble from the first lap and the 917 unable to keep up the the pace of the well driven Ford. Behind the six 908s, the 312P and the Ickx Mirage, the GT40 settled down to racing smaller capacity cars for a top ten position while keeping a look out for Bonnier who was carving back through the field after a pit stop at the end of the first lap.

The Lola got close to the Ford but the latter ran significantly further to its first fuel stop, far enough to go through on two rather than three stops. The Ford was still in front when the T70 rolled to a halt soon after half distance with a broken u.j. on the left hand driveshaft. The GT40 ran out the Group 4 winner, three laps behind the winning 908, one lap ahead of the 917. The 312P retired while 908s filled all the spaces on the final results sheet above the Ford.

Le Mans (F) June 16
24 Heures du Mans
Bonnier/Gregory Q:10/R:NR

As at Francorchamps, the entry of the 917 gave Sports-Prototype racing a new complexion. Le Mans is about sheer speed and that the 917 had, though it took a lot of work to make it driveable. In essence, the car had to be run slightly pitched towards the front to make it anything like stable on the straight, and it still used a lot of road as it shot the Mulsanne at around 215m.p.h. It wasn't anywhere near as stable as the 7.0 litre cars of '66 and could not take the kink flat out.

Nevertheless, it was the only car capable of topping 200m.p.h. Stommelen clocked 202.9 seconds for pole, Elford put a second example next on the grid and the only other car that could get within seven seconds of pole was Siffert's special long tail 908/2 spyder.

There were a total of three 917s, including the first customer example for John Woolfe while only the Filipinetti Lola represented the T70 force. The JWA GT40s were out again, while three other examples included the Kelleners/Joest car. Group 6 comprised the bulk of the serious runners, Porsche running three 908 coupes in addition to the Siffert/Redman spyder while Ferrari had two 312Ps with new coupe bodies, Alpine had four regular-style cars and Matra had four cars only one of which was a coupe.

As expected the works 917s and the long tail 908/2 ran away at the start while tragically Woolfe lost control of his 917 under braking for White House on the first lap, losing his life in the ensuing accident. That accident knocked out one 312P coupe but in any case the rebodied Ferrari was disappointingly slow. As Porsche took an early grip on the race the T70 ran in the lower part of the top ten, looking strong for seven hours. Indeed, at quarter distance it ran ahead of the JWA team, holding a steady sixth position. Then cracked cylinder heads slowed it. These were replaced, as were gaskets, valves and brake discs.

Alas, having taken three hours hard toil by the mechanics, the car's Chevrolet engine failed on the Mulsanne shortly after half distance. The race had meanwhile fallen into the grip of the Elford/Ahrens 917, the sister car and the 908/2 spyder having run into trouble. The 917 sailed on towards success until 11.00am. Sunday when its transmission failed. Its demise left the JWA GT40 of Ickx/Oliver in the lead, chased by Porsche's last surviving hope, a delayed 908 coupe in

Diary continues on page 90

later commented to the author: "all Porsche
coupes up to the Osterreichring had a tail with
a rounded rear part. In the wind tunnel the aerodynamics were much better. But previous cars
had too little power, with the 917 suddenly we
had too much. Aerodynamic stability was suddenly a very important factor. We saw from this
modification that... reducing top speed and gaining stability was the right way to go..."

As Broadley had appreciated some three years
earlier, low drag could not be everything. Porsche duly produced a refined high tail body for

the 917 that took its drag co-efficient from 0.400
to 0.464. This tail looked very much like the
familiar tail of the T70 coupe...

Ironically, this was the season in which the
Formula One constructors started to get real
work out of wings. Prior to a mid season ban on
remote mounted aerofoils, downforce went as
high as 350kg. (720lb.) - around half the car's
own weight - at maximum speed (say 165m.p.h).
This complemented a further increase in the
width of the flat tread tyres now in use. However, some cars suffered suspension failure as a

the hands of Hans Herrmann/Gerard Larrousse. Of the other serious runners, Matra had shone but had failed to sustain its attack on the 908 ranks (though it had three cars still running) while the second JWA GT40 lay third.

At the end, the 908 coupe failed to dislodge the Ford by a few yards: the race was a great success for JWA, with first and third while the steady Joest/Kelleners GT40 backed its Monza and Nurburgring class wins with a steady sixth overall behind two of the three Matra survivors.

Watkins Glen (USA) July 6
Watkins Glen 6 Hours
Bonnier/Muller .... Q: 4/R:NR

After Le Mans the Porsche factory officially pulled out of sports car racing for the balance of the season, having come to an agreement for JWA to run its cars in 1970. The factory R&D department that had been running the effort had other pressing work but those in the company closely involved with racing ensured the 908s continued to see out the season, albeit through private teams. Thus, in the USA three factory prepared 908/2s came out in familiar hands under the banner of Porsche Salzburg and Tony Dean Racing. In opposition Matra had two spyders while JWA had its Cosworth-Mirage converted to spyder trim, leaving Group 4 to the T70 and the Kelleners/Joest GT40.

Bonnier set a good practice time, lapping in 71.1 seconds compared to Siffert's 908 pole of 70.3 seconds, whereas the GT40 could not better 74.3 seconds. Bonnier slotted into a good third place at the start, following Siffert and the quick (front row) Matra of Servoz-Gavin while

Elford's 908/2 gave him chase. After ten minutes it started to drizzle and Elford's Dunlop 'intermediates' gave him an advantage over Bonnier's Goodyear dry tyres. Indeed, the 908/2 also quickly disposed of the Matra, which likewise was on dries.

The Lola stopped for wets and, as Matra found trouble, took up station behind the 908/2 trio with the Mirage and the GT40 proving to be no threat. Bonnier drove for over three hours then handed to Muller. Alas, four laps into his stint the engine failed. Porsche finished first, second and third while the GT40 took another Group 4 win, albeit beaten by the recovering Matra of Servoz-Gavin and Rodriguez.

Osterreichring (A) August 10
Austrian Grand Prix (1000km.)
Bonnier/Muller .... Q: 2/R:2
Piper/Quester .... Q: 9/R:NR

In Austria Porsche continued to race factory cars through private teams and brought out the 917 once more in view of the high speed nature of the sweeping new Osterreichring circuit that rolled through Alpine foothills. Three 908/2s and two 917s were unloaded, the big cars running under the banners of Karl von Wendt and David Piper, both of whom had options to buy at a later date. Piper also had his green Lola and this he was driving with Dieter Quester, leaving the difficult 917 to the factory pilots.

Principal rivals to the 908s in Group 6 were the Ickx/Oliver open Mirage - now better sorted - the Servoz-Gavin/Rodriguez Matra and three T33-3 models from Autodelta. Group 4 contained only the 917s and the Piper and Filipinetti T70s as serious runners. Muller crumpled both left side corners of the Filipinetti car in practice but Bonnier still managed to put it on the front row of the grid, second only to Ickx who had the Mirage flying. Servoz-Gavin was next quickest, ahead of Siffert in the 917 and Ignazio Giunti in the fastest T33-3.

Siffert was driving the 917 reluctantly, since it was still uncivilised an here was little quicker than the 908 However, Porsche was keen to continu its development with a view to 1970 an racing it this weekend was one means t that end. The opening laps saw tremendous tussle between Ickx and Siffert, Denis Jenkinson observing in Moto Sport: "the enormous power advantag of the Porsche being offset by the fact i is still a handful in the corners and keep its driver very busy, whereas the Mirag was far superior on handling".

Behind the lead battle, Gregory in 908/2 led Bonnier, who was busy keeping Servoz-Gavin, Giunti and the othe 908s at bay, the second 917 of Attwood Redman uncompetitive in the hands o the former. An unscheduled stop fo Gregory after 150 kilometres elevated Bonnier to third. Then came the first pi stops and significantly the 917s were in first, after 35 of 170 laps whereas Bonnie and the Matra stayed out the longest, fo 43 laps. At that rate they alone could g through on three stops. And the Porsch refuelling was slow, that of Matra quick Rodriguez taking the Matra out ahead o Muller in the T70 who in turn was ahead of Kurt Ahrens in the thirsty Siffert Porsche, the Mirage still leading.

Ahrens went well in the 917 to work i back up to second place before handing over to Siffert whereas Muller fell back from the leaders. After the second round of pit stops the Mirage led comfortably from the Matra and the 917 with the Lola a lap down on all three in fourth place. Bonnier rejoined close behind Siffert on the road, Jenkinson reporting "Bonnier was in great form, the Lola cornering so much better than the 917 that he was able not only to keep pace, but actually overtake, thus putting himself on the same lap as Siffert".

After 99 laps the Mirage retired with broken steering, throwing the race wide open: Siffert was gaining on Servoz-

Diary continues on page 92

The Penske T70 at Sebring. World Championship race victory second time in a row might have been expecting too much but the car led in convincing style before its suspension broke.

consequence of the download.

Wing technology was not seized upon by the World Championship for Manufacturers runners. Ferrari had fitted a big wing to its '68 Can Am car but kept its '69 3.0 litre spyder free of such a drag-inducing device. Then Technical Director Mauro Forghieri subsequently explained to the author: "Endurance racing is a compromise between performance, reliability, fuel consumption and driveability. Lower cornering loads are less stressful. Fuel consumption was a major consideration, particularly as the refuelling had to be through small diameter pipes without pressure. And top speed was very significant with so much traffic around in the races".

By the time Porsche had tamed its 917 it was too late for the model to show its true potential in 1969 World Championship races. Of course, in original form it had come close to winning Le Mans, the task for which it had been designed, and it had won at the Osterreichring. For its part, the T70 Mk.IIIB had worked well at Daytona and Sebring, aside from its obvious top form at Francorchamps and the Osterreichring, leaving question marks over its potential at Watkins Glen and in Italy.

No doubt about it, the T70 was not suited to the World title bouts at Brands Hatch and the Nurburgring where the new breed of ultra light, manoeuvrable spyder shone, nor was it anywhere near the pace at Le Mans given the sledgehammering power of the new 917.

In the USA, the professionalism of the Penske team shone through in terms of preparation, management, race engineering and driving abil-

Overleaf the Bonnier/ Muller T70 is seen leading the Siffert/ Ahrens 917 in the great Osterreichring showdown. The T70 gave away over 100 horsepower to the 917 but was not overshadowed by any means...

ity. Donohue, Parsons and Bucknum could get the best out of the car and kept it up with the 908 coupes at Daytona and with the 908/2 and Ferrari 312P spyders at Sebring. Penske's meticulous preparation was second to none, but that did not avoid serious delays en route to victory at Daytona and it did not stop suspension failure putting the car out at Sebring. Interestingly, Penske toyed with fuel injection at Daytona (employing the simple Hilborn Indy Car system) but reverted to carburettors for Sebring.

In spite of the setbacks, the Penske performances did suggest that the Philly team could have taken the T70 on to further success in World Championship races. Monza, even the Madonie, certainly Francorchamps, Le Mans, Watkins Glen, the Osterreichring. On those circuits Donohue would have been up there with the best of them, a favourite for victory with either of his co-drivers... and luck on his side. There was no chassis weakness that Penske would not have eradicated and though the Small Block Chevrolet was not 100% dependable on pump petrol, it would have held together enough times to have seriously upset Porsche, Ferrari and JWA...

But that is mere speculation. The fact is that the Bonnier/Filipinetti car continued the campaign on the budget of an amateur team and inevitably chassis and engine preparation for it and all the other similarly shoestring European teams was wanting. Again this season the T70 was a popular car in non-championship racing, taking many wins, often in the hands of top rank drivers. For example, Redman won the Nor-

Gavin while Bonnier was gaining on Siffert. Five laps later the Matra spun out and the 5.0 litre cars led the race, the 917 still the best part of a lap ahead and third place in dispute some way behind the T70.

Siffert handed to Ahrens once again after 118 laps and the engine was reluctant to start. Bonnier went into the lead, though due in soon for the T70's third stop. When that was done Muller found himself half a lap down on Ahrens with 40 laps left to run and a non-stop drive in prospect whereas the Porsche would need more fuel. Ahrens was urged on and increased the gap. According to Jenkinson: "Muller could not rise to the situation. He was not happy on the fast blind curves, and his practice accident had detuned him a bit, so nothing could be done".

So it was that the 917 lapped the T70, then Ahrens swooped into the pits. Jenkinson: "The tension was great, for the slightest slip could throw the race away, and it was ironical to think of the whole computerised and electronically controlled Porsche team, with the pits knee-deep in engineers and mechanics being brought into such a state of nervous twitch by two private drivers controlled by two mechanics, Bonnier's wife and a friend!".

This time the 917 fired instantly, Siffert made a drag racing start and he resumed with almost a minute in hand. The margin at the finish was 67 seconds. However, the T70 beat the second 917, which had not found the pace of the Siffert/Ahrens car. Meanwhile, the Piper/Quester T70 had retired from mid field with overheating, thoroughly overshadowed.

isring in Sid Taylor's car. However, a number of other T70s entered for the event expired with engine failure and Motor Sport correspondent Denis Jenkinson was moved to remark: "it would seem that 200 miles is still a long way to race a Chevrolet engine, when it is basically a standard unit prepared by small time tuners".

Although the Mk.IIIB suffered an early overheating problem, the model was basically sound. A GM Tech backed Penske bid would have been something; Bonnier's World Championship bid was something else. Sporting is the word that comes to mind. Bonnier had gone well at Daytona (before co-driver Norinder hit the wall) and Filipinetti regular Muller went surprisingly well at the Targa Florio, giving a real virtuoso performance first time around the Madonie, one strong enough to put the big machine in an eye-opening third place overall. Before that ill-starred adventure, early race problems for all the quick T70 drivers at Monza had stopped the Mk.IIIB showing its true paces on the far faster Italian circuit.

Monza was an intriguing confrontation: Porsche ran a low drag coupe, Ferrari its regular low frontal area, higher drag co-efficient and more powerful spyder. Neither the 350b.h.p. Porsche nor the 420b.h.p. Ferrari had a clear cut advantage. The Chevrolet-Lola was heavier than the Porsche 908 and had more drag but, like the Ferrari it had a significant power advantage. Logically, it should have kept pace in view of the nature of the banked plus high speed road circuit.

Clearly, however, the latest Mk.IIIB was in its element through the sweeps of Francorchamps. There its trade off of drag for downforce was optimum. This year at Francorchamps Hawkins - as in '67 - emphatically demonstrated what Lola's coupe was capable of, even if Mk.IIIB stalwarts Bonnier and Muller could not.

Nevertheless, the final fling for the Fillipinetti duo at the new Osterreichring was fair reward for their perseverance. Such a shame, though, that Bonnier was not backed by Donohue: that combination might well have beaten the 917, thus ending the T70 Coupe story on a rousing note. Instead, the car pre-ordained to end its career had its kill.

"The T70 project was a landmark in the history of Lola," Eric Broadley confirms, "the whole T70 saga was important to us." Of course, the Can Am car achieved far more in the way of major success than the Coupe, the subject of this book. However, the Coupe was an excellent car for the privateer and achieved much success away from World Championship races. "The Coupe was a good, simple car at the time," Broadley reflects, "it looked nice and it worked quite well."

Work well it did, having the right blend of simplicity and sophistication. It is worth remembering that the T70 series was one of the first examples of a monocoque machine being offered for general sale. Indeed, the forerunner of the Coupe, the Lola GT of '62, had a monocoque chassis the same year as the pioneering Lotus 25 Grand Prix car.

Of course, the Lola GT didn't have a full monocoque, as Broadley points out: it had tubular constructions front and rear and monocoque-style sill boxes carrying the fuel. "That was a pretty obvious configuration," Broadley reflects, explaining that it was a logical means of saving weight while producing a very stiff structure.

After the Lola GT Broadley was involved with the Ford GT40 which carried a full monocoque, then he produced the T70, again with a full monocoque. However, as we have seen, the GT40 had a much stiffer monocoque than the T70: comparative figures are 10,000lb. ft. per degree for the Ford, 3,200 for the Lola. Broadley emphasises that the Ford's steel monocoque was exceedingly heavy, its significant weight penalty to no real advantage: "the Ford was probably far stiffer than was necessary at that stage of the game."

Broadley recalls Lola making its own calipers for the Can Am car: "the calipers available at that time were not rigid enough. Since the T70 brakes were outside of the wheels, we could have a bigger bridge for the caliper." The bigger bridge, being more substantial, was stiffer. Of course, in the mid to late Sixties technology was changing fast, soon ventilated discs arrived and so did wider wheels and tyres and with aerodynamic development as well the T70 MkIII Coupe of '67 matured into the T70 MkIIIB of '69.

"The IIIB was a natural progression," says Broadley, adding: "it was a lot quicker than the Mk III." However, he looks upon its changed aerodynamics as "not a dramatic jump – a logical progression." Aside from aerodynamic improvements: "it had wider tyres, better suspension – with different geometry – and a better monocoque. It was a better car right through."

Of course, what both versions lacked was the right engine. There were high hopes for the Aston Martin engine, sadly unfulfilled. "That engine was at an early stage of its development," Broadley recalls, "I suspect that it was not working properly in a car."

Broadley recalls the first time he drove an Aston Martin engined Coupe, on the road between the workshop and the circuit at Le Mans. "I was shocked at the vibration level. It was awful." Broadley agrees that a two plane 90 degree V8 should be smooth running, and the Aston's abnormal vibration perhaps helps explain the crankshaft damper failure on the Irwin/de Klerk car early in the race.

Incidentally, Broadley recalls that at the start of the race a young mechanic came up to him, white as a sheet and shaking: he had forgotten to stow the spare wheel in the car. "We concocted a charade to try to get it in at the first pit stop without the official on our pit noticing," Broadley relates, "but I don't think he was convinced." In any case the car was already in engine trouble...

Surtees subsequently switched to the Chevrolet V8. "It became obvious that a lot of work was needed on the Aston engine," Broadley reflects, "it didn't produce the right horsepower given that it was a double overhead cam engine and it was not reliable either." Not that the Chevrolet was the ideal replacement. In the USA it thrived on high octane fuel – 108 RON plus – in sprint races such as the Can Am series; endurance races in Europe on the mandatory lower octane fuel were another matter altogether.

"Detonation was a continuous problem on European fuel," Broadley reports: "the Chevrolet had a big piston and a combustion chamber shape that was not ideal. Every time you stripped an engine there were signs of detonation." Broadley speculates that the detonation problem aggravated the head gasket weakness that characterised the engine's European life. "It was a continuous battle to hold the gaskets in," Broadley sighs, "that was one of the biggest reliability problems." He also points to the effect of the big, heavy valves on the valve train: "everything fatigued."

Alas, there was no real alternative engine – "we were pretty much stuck with the Chevrolet. We looked at doing something in '67, then they changed the rules. The Coupe never had a decent engine so it never became a world beater."

On the other hand, the Coupe was an extremely important car in terms of the overall development of the Sports Prototype. In the Sixties Broadley had an advanced appreciation of the importance of downforce and this shone through the T70 project. It was not that he underestimated the importance of drag, though, and initially he had been as reluctant as anyone else to resort to spoilers. The first spyder rolled out without a spoiler.

"With the Roadster shape we were trying to reduce lift over the top," Broadley explains, "initially avoiding the use of spoilers. We wanted a level tail to avoid lift, but smooth for low drag."

However, it was quickly discovered that the car would be better off with a spoiler. Broadley recalls an early Group 7 race at Silverstone in the wet, Surtees driving the prototype T70 spyder with a clean tail. "John was very quick but it was obvious that the car was light at the back." In response Broadley wanted to improvise a spoiler. Surtees would have none of it. "In the race he spun maybe ten times on the wet track. That convinced him that a spoiler would be a good thing."

Indeed, it was at this stage that Broadley came to appreciate just how effective a spoiler could be on the back of a spyder. "The difference in lap times was amazing – you could get two to three seconds a lap." However, while the first few inches of spoiler were extremely effective, there was little to be gained going higher – the drag shot up for no significant increase in downforce.

Broadley notes: "spoilers were good when there was a good horizontal surface with the air attached." That was the case with the T70 spyder but contemporary coupes tended to lose the airflow behind the cockpit. The conventional sloping back helped pull the air in the right direction to minimise drag but at the same time accelerated the flow across the tail, causing low pressure over a large surface area, hence typically there was a lot of lift.

Broadley had driven sports cars with a low drag shape and knew all about low pressure over the tail. "Cars with a sloping back and no spoiler had tremendous lift off the top. That made them diabolical to drive – a real white knuckle, tightrope job. It wasn't just the lift but the variable lift, and the variable breakaway point of the air along the sides of the body, in yaw and in crosswinds..."

This was what Porsche later discovered: a powerful low drag car can be seriously unstable even in a straight line. Broadley appreciated the importance of stability to all aspects of the car's performance – under acceleration, flat out, under braking and in the corners. It was this that guided him in the shape of the MkIII Coupe.

"The high back put a lot of drag on the car but it was so much quicker through the corners and under braking that the drag became irrelevant, except at Le Mans." Broadley admits that the Coupe's shape was largely, "feel- based on previous experience. We didn't know if we would get significant downforce at the back, we were really just combating lift. From driving myself I knew the horrid effects of lift over the body."

In the mid Sixties downforce was something that engineers were wary of. "Downforce could quickly overwhelm the car, overloading the tall tyres, squashing them. In the mid Sixties we found that adding more and more downforce didn't make the car go more quickly." This helps explain why others did not rush out and copy the Chaparral wing in '66. Lola won that year's Can Am Championship over Chaparral without resort to a wing and in '67 Sports-Prototype racing the Chaparral's wing was as unique as it was unfamiliar.

"There was a fair amount of scepticism about

the wing," Broadley recalls. "Funny Texan ideas. People tended to think that it wasn't racing car stuff – wings are for aeroplanes. The rest of us were a bit conservative. We all started thinking about it, but it took a while. There were a lot of unknowns and we couldn't stop work and develop new things very easily. We all had very small operations at that time."

Broadley points out that at Lola in the mid Sixties, "we were stretched. We had to make cars and go racing at weekends. We didn't have the spare time to respond very quickly. Jim Hall had his own test track – no one else was in that situation."

Broadley agrees that in '66/'77 the wing was ahead of tyre technology, though he says Goodyear was close behind Hall. The main problem for everyone was that it was not simply a case of bolting any old wing onto a car, it was a big leap into the dark. For example, there was the question, should the wing feed directly into the uprights, as in the case of the Chaparral, or should it be attached to the body?

Broadley: "I suspect it would have been best to have put a wing on the sprung mass. The advantage of putting it on the uprights is that it doesn't then affect the spring rates needed for slow and fast corners. But the disadvantage is lift over the body, then you have to start putting spoilers on to hold the body down."

Of course, Chaparral found that at high speed, it had to create lift at the nose via its intriguing trap door. In general terms, downforce at the back calls for downforce at the front to keep a balance. Broadley explains that at this time, downforce at the front of a sports car was unwelcome, not only because it pitched up the back of the car, adding to lift at the rear.

"Downforce at the front unsettled the car," Broadley reveals, pointing out that the cars at this time had narrow tyres which called for a soft, supple suspension. Having soft springing the cars experienced quite a lot of pitch and roll while the narrow front tyres couldn't take a lot of load input. There was necessarily a lot of wheel movement at the front where downforce was inappropriate.

"It was a problem stabilising the whole thing – you didn't want the car to be pointy." Broadley emphasises that there was a very

subtle balance to be struck, with ideally: "a little float at the front and stability at the back."

It was for this reason that the cars at this time were run raked, the tail riding perhaps one and a half inches higher than the nose. This made the car more difficult to set up, Broadley notes. Interestingly, he speculates that with a large area of raked undertray and an inward curved lower nose panel, there may well have been an element of ground effect. Air was logically accelerating under the nose, between the front wheels where there was consequently low pressure. On the other hand, the effect of air packing under the relatively high nose inlet was to create high pressure, as Ford discovered.

Broadley says that the original design study for the GT40 specifically incorporated a pure venturi shape running the entire length of the car. Thus, it had a very high nose and a rising tail, the former turning out to be impractical due to the effect of air packing under it. "But they were on the right lines," Broadley acknowledges.

In the final analysis, by the standard of '67 the T70 Coupe was extremely advanced in terms of aerodynamics, without going beyond the constraints of contemporary chassis and tyre technology. As tyres progressed cars could carry more download and as more was added at the back, there needed to be appropriate downforce at the front to balance it. Throughout, it was a question of balancing downforce at the front – which is relatively easy to obtain – to that generated at the rear. Hence the transition from MkIII body shape to MkIIIB body shape.

How much downforce the Coupe generated in either guise is anyone's guess, for all the talk of wind tunnel testing there was little truly enlightening research at this stage. For example, Broadley says that in '67 the MIRA tunnel "had a boundary layer two feet thick. In reality the downforce we had might have been twice what was measured there."

Broadley suspects that even the original MkIII might have attained as much as half its own weight in downforce at 180m.p.h. – which is clearly why Hawkins found it so controllable at Spa Francorchamps, unlike Siffert two years later with the original low drag Porsche 917...

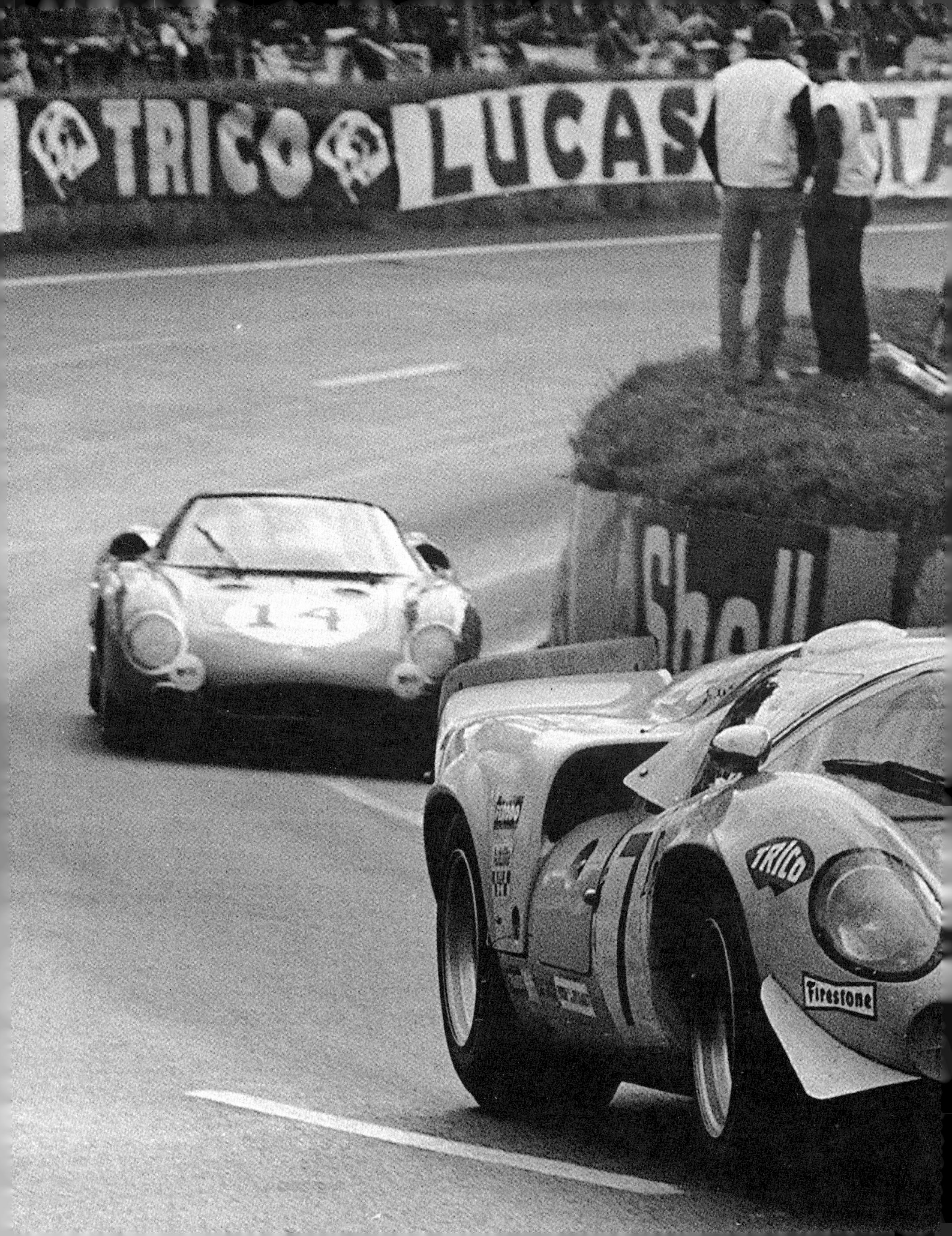
TRICO
TRICO
LUCAS
14
TRICO
Firestone